Get

SAFe®

Now

A Lightning Introduction to the Most Popular Scaling Framework on Agile

##

Revision 1.4, December 2016

##

Also by Mohammed Musthafa Soukath Ali, available at leading online retailers:

1. Scrum Narrative and PSM Exam Guide (#1 Best Seller in smashwords.com).

2. The Professional Scrum Product Owner: Guide to Pass PSPO 1 Certification.

3. A Pocket Guide to Passing Professional Scrum Master (PSM 1).

4. A Lightning Introduction to Scrum.

Editor-in-Chief: **Samantha Mason**

##

Preface

The Scaled Agile Framework® (SAFe®) is owned and overseen by Scaled Agile, Inc. SAFe® was created in response to the needs of companies that wanted to use their small and effective Agile Teams for larger development efforts. Traditional software development processes, such as waterfall, increase the prediction-related risks by promoting detailed upfront planning that require long-term assumptions. The Agile Teams do not rely on long-term predictions. Instead, they plan shorter iterations, collaborate with focus to complete the iterations, learn and adjust along the way, and incrementally reach the goal. The Agile Teams themselves have proven to be promising alternatives to the traditional software development team hierarchy. These Agile Teams are appropriately sized to plan, communicate, and respond faster than traditional development teams. They are cross-functional with a mix of required skills to independently complete their work. They are self-organized to decide how to complete their work to meet a common goal which allows quick decisions along the way.

When companies, or enterprises as they are called in SAFe®, tried to scale these Agile Teams to larger efforts, which had many interdependent teams, several questions arose. The questions include

- What are the roles and responsibilities of the organization's management?

- How to align the Agile Teams to the corporate strategies?

- How to cascade these strategies to the hundreds of Agile Teams?

- How can different business owners, who have different needs that impact the same set of Agile Teams, collaborate?

- How to integrate the work performed by different Agile Teams?

- How to integrate support teams like Technology Architecture, User Experience, Project Management Office, etc.?

- How to align the upstream business functions, such as portfolio management and program management, with the Agile Teams?

SAFe® tries to answer these questions by providing a framework of levels, work backlogs, roles, and activities along with a set of values and a set of principles.

How do I know if we should implement SAFe®?

SAFe® is intended for large teams that cannot avoid inherent dependencies. Wherever feasible, find opportunities to form smaller independent teams which are better because they have clear product ownership, less coordination overhead, and rapid decision-making enablers. These small teams can Inspect and Adapt using one of the simple Agile frameworks such as Scrum. However, in the event that the business needs require large solutions or products involving many highly dependent teams working together in order to produce the value, consider implementing SAFe®.

What if we decide that we don't need to implement SAFe®, can we skip learning about it?

SAFe® principles and values can be considered for any team. Even after the analysis and decision-making that SAFe® is not needed for a given context, there are valuable elements of SAFe® that can be applied by any team including those using Scrum, Extreme Programming (XP), etc. In particular the principles such as using an economic framework for decision-making, visualization of work, continuous flow of value, common cadence between different teams, reducing the batch size, etc. can be implemented within other frameworks.

Attention: This book is not a comprehensive guide to SAFe® nor does it explain every nuance of SAFe®. Instead, it purposefully spends most of the sections explaining the 'most common start-up approach of SAFe®' taken by many organizations. This involves understanding the building blocks of SAFe®, scaling the current Agile Teams into a team called Agile Release Train (ART), launching the ART to deliver quick results, and then inspecting the need for subsequent scaling. Although one can finish this book in one sitting, the author recommends spending enough time to understand each concept, rereading sections if necessary. The intent is to get the best basic understanding of SAFe® in the least amount of time. The basic but holistic knowledge acquired through this book should be augmented later by exploring SAFe®'s "*Big Picture*."

##

Table of Contents

##

An Overview

The SAFe® is built on the principles from Lean, Agile, and Systems Thinking. This framework helps enterprises to deliver value in the sustainably shortest lead time by optimizing the end-to-end product development workflow, reducing the behavior to accumulate the work into large batches, and eliminating the delays inherent in large developments.

You may have noticed in the previous paragraph that SAFe® introduces a lot of new terminology. In addition, SAFe® has multiple perspectives to understand. The following is a list of different perspectives of SAFe®.

Perspective	Description
A software development framework	SAFe® is a framework composed of levels, roles, work backlogs, and activities. It is flexible and allows an organization to pick and choose a custom implementation.
A Lean-Agile leadership culture	For an entire enterprise to enjoy all the benefits of SAFe®, it is essential that the leaders and management drive the SAFe® implementation of a Lean-Agile way of working.
A way to scale Agile for larger enterprises	SAFe® answers questions and provides a solution for scaling Agile Teams to an enterprise that may have several interdependent teams.

The seemingly obvious way to learn SAFe® is to start with the Scaled Agile website. All the elements of SAFe® are captured in one single "*Big Picture*" at http://www.scaledagileframework.com. At first glance, it looks structured and neatly defined, but due to its size, new terminology, and multiple perspectives, the first introduction to the "*Big Picture*" or a SAFe® training can be overwhelming. While SAFe®'s "*Big Picture*" is thorough and complete, it is heavy for first-time readers. Before exploring the "*Big Picture*" or going into every tiny detail of SAFe®, a quick and lightweight narrative of SAFe® is beneficial. This book provides a narrative of the most valuable elements of SAFe®. This book

- Narrates the SAFe® concepts in simple terms.

- Uses visuals to drive the concepts.

- Provides real world examples.

- Uses Active Learning to commit the new knowledge to memory. Active Learning is not just the passive reading of content, but it provides frequent pauses to absorb the new information. In Active Learning, after presenting new content, related questions will be presented. Answering these questions requires thinking, analyzing, and inferring the meaning of what was just read.

Here is an example of Active Learning. Let us say you read the statement: 'SAFe® is a development framework for each portfolio in an enterprise.' Immediately after, you are provided with a related question.

----------Question- 1----------

'Portfolio' is a SAFe® specific term.

a) True

b) False

-------Answer-------

SAFe® does talk about the Portfolio Level. However, 'portfolio' is a general industry term. Every company or enterprise usually has set of portfolios for their management convenience. Correct answer is 'b.'

----------Question- 1----------

You may have noticed that the question shifts you from passive reading into active thinking because you need to answer the question. This exercise makes you go over what you just read once again and anchors it into your memory.

When you say 'framework,' what does it mean?

Is SAFe® a proven approach?

A framework is a set of guidelines and success patterns to approach a problem. Frameworks, however, are not very prescriptive about which tools and techniques to use. SAFe®, which is only a framework not a prescription, provides the flexibility to customize the process to best fit the enterprise. For example, one of the problems in applying Agile in a large enterprise is how to allocate the funds. SAFe® recommends a funding pattern called *"Lean-Agile Budgeting,"* which will be discussed in more detail later. In a nutshell, SAFe® allows the enterprise to define its own techniques for sub-budgeting areas such as calculating business benefits and finding approval criteria within the confines of *"Lean-Agile Budgeting."*

As for the question 'Is SAFe® a proven approach?' Scaled Agile states that "over 60% of the Fortune 100 U.S. companies have certified SAFe® practitioners and consultants already on site." Follow this link http://www.scaledagileframework.com/case-studies for a list of 25+ case studies documenting the proven adoption of SAFe®.

##

Portfolio and Flow

Scaled Agile provides a formal definition of SAFe® - "*SAFe® is an online, freely revealed knowledge base of proven success patterns for implementing Lean-Agile software and systems development at enterprise scale.*" But this definition is broad. How can we understand SAFe® better?

Compared to other Agile software development frameworks, SAFe® is distinct in

- **Where it fits** in an enterprise, and

- How much it enables the continuous **flow** of company strategies to end values such as useful software for the customer.

SAFe® visualizes every enterprise (SAFe®'s term for a company), as a collection of portfolios. Per SAFe®, each portfolio of an enterprise needs an implementation of SAFe®.

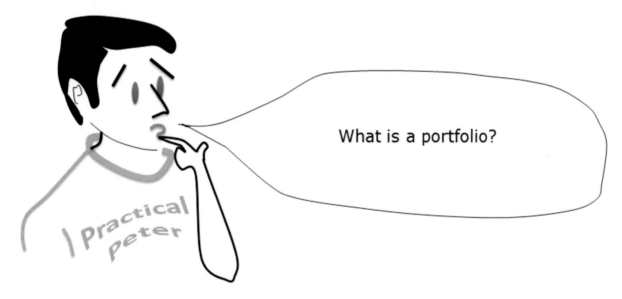

A portfolio indicates a group of business units in an enterprise. Enterprises group their business units into portfolios for the convenience of defining investments and setting and tracking targets. There is no universal rule on how to form portfolios. Different enterprises can form portfolios based on different themes. Some may have product centric grouping. For example, an insurance company can have a Life portfolio, Healthcare portfolio, and Property portfolio. Some may have channel centric grouping. For example, a retail company can have Stores, On-line, and Warehouse. Per SAFe®, each portfolio needs one implementation of SAFe®. In other words, SAFe® fits in at the Portfolio Level. Unlike many other Agile frameworks, SAFe® applies holistic thinking to software development. Rather than treating the software development effort as a standalone endeavor, it visualizes it as part of a portfolio of an enterprise. This is based on the SAFe® principle "*Apply systems thinking.*"

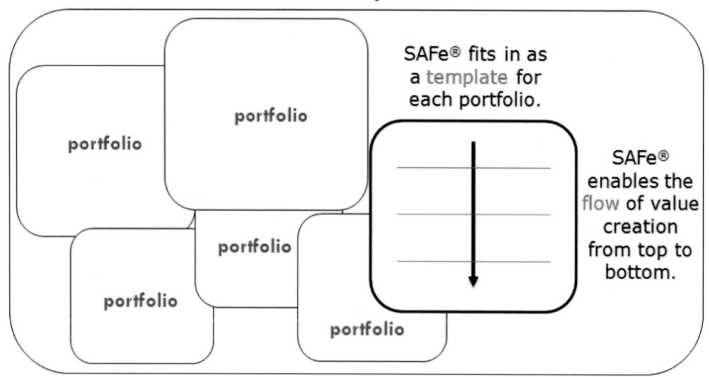

An Enterprise

portfolio

portfolio

portfolio

portfolio

portfolio

SAFe® fits in as a template for each portfolio.

SAFe® enables the flow of value creation from top to bottom.

Fig. 1- SAFe® Portfolio and Flow

The second distinguishing aspect of SAFe® is that it improves the flow of value, that is to say solutions and software systems, from the strategic level to the end customers. Usually enterprises plan and execute projects to convert business needs into software systems. However, the projects may not be the right vehicles to continuously flow the business needs into the software systems. Projects pass through many checkpoints, each of which requires making informed decisions in order to move to the next phase. In addition to these checkpoints, projects also face day-to-day issues that may require quick and localized decisions. Traditionally projects are set up with a strict hierarchy for decision-making. Project teams must often wait for someone higher up in the organization to make the decisions. This results in idle time, late decisions, and inappropriate decisions which did not consider localized information. All of these impede the continuous flow of progress.

A project is a time-bound activity to create something of value to the enterprise. For example, an Insurance company may initiate a project to upgrade its old system of insurance policy application administration to a modern technology. Since projects are large initiatives that consume investments, resources, and time, they undergo various approval steps within a company from the funding phase to the actual implementation. Company executives, who know about the enterprise's long-term vision and strategies, provide the funding approval. For the enterprise to realize the benefits, these projects need to be completed as soon as possible so users can access the project outcome. For the enterprise to exploit market opportunities, the project outcome needs to quickly reach the market. As discussed earlier, project teams often wait for decisions throughout the project life cycle and incur delays.

----------Question- 2----------

Traditional projects emphasize

  a) Continuous value delivery.

  b) Scope decomposition into small batch sizes.

  c) Multiple start and stop points.

  d) A phase-gated process.

  -------Answer-------

Traditional projects do not enable the flow. They incur start-stop-start delays. Correct answers are 'c' and 'd.'

----------Question- 2----------

SAFe® helps to improve the flow of value from the strategic level to the customers. SAFe® uses two primary means to do this. First, it eliminates too much centralization of project initiatives at the Enterprise Level. Instead SAFe® gives the empowerment to the next lower level, which is the Portfolio Level, to define the initiatives and approve them. Second, it defines clear authority levels within a portfolio so people can make quicker decisions using their authority rather than waiting for decisions from the top.

As an example, let's use a bank that has three business lines - Lending, Deposit, and Advice. Traditionally, the bank scopes the strategies into projects. The projects are executed using some software development process and are then delivered.

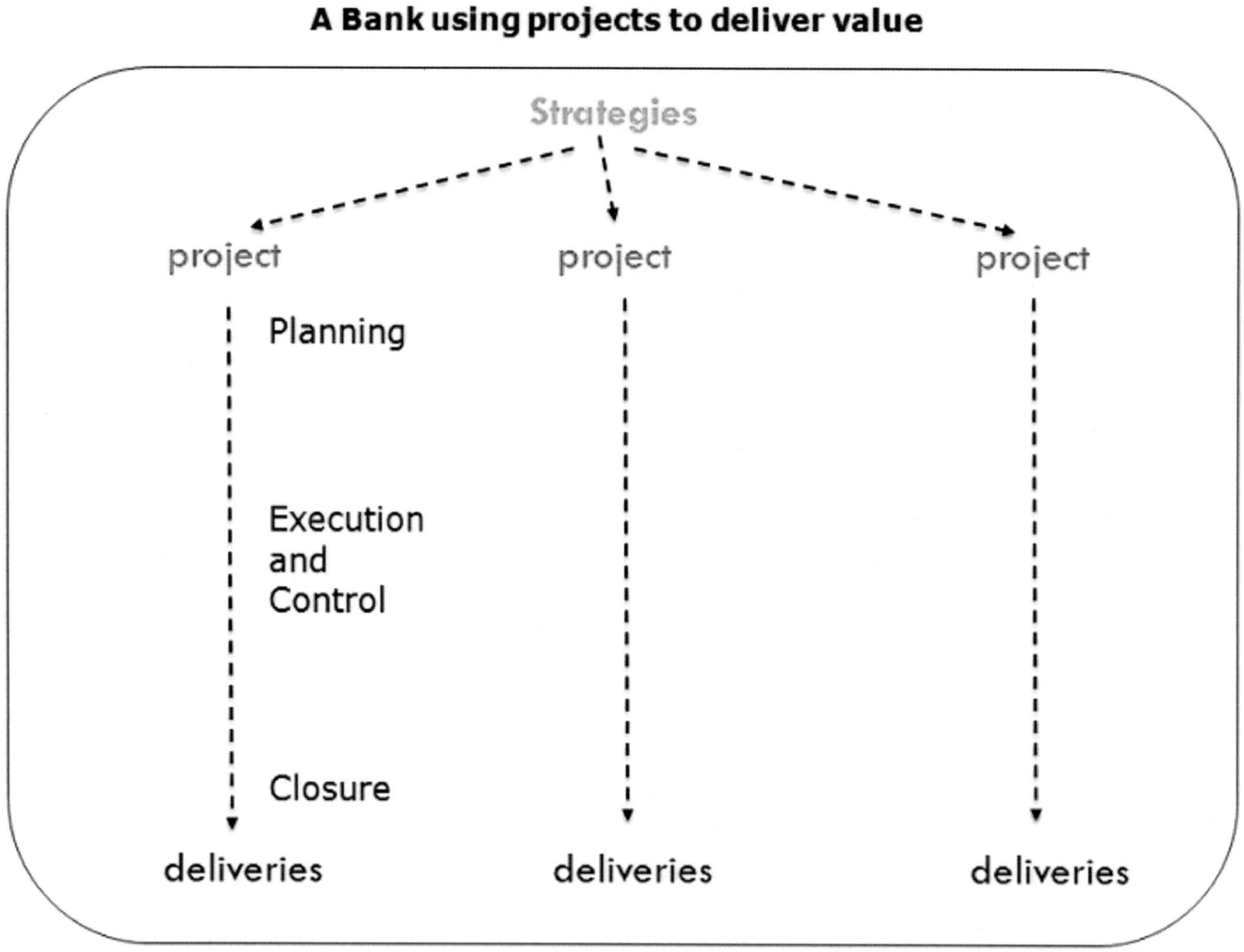

A Bank using projects to deliver value

Fig. 2- Strategies delivered through projects

If SAFe® is applied to the Deposits projects at this bank, it may look like Fig. 3. The picture shows the benefits that can be expected from this implementation. Notice that SAFe® reduces the problem of too much centralization by removing the traditional projects. It empowers the teams in the next level within the portfolio with more authority. It also promotes close collaboration within the portfolio and hence improves the flow. The net outcome is a quick and continuous delivery of value.

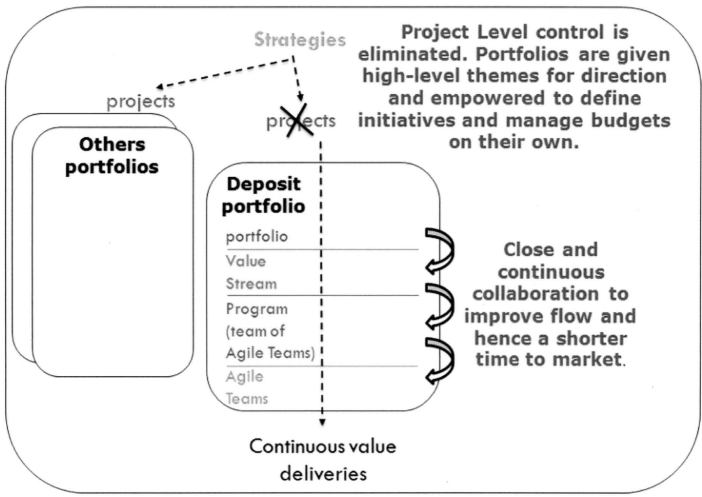

Fig. 3- Using SAFe® constructs instead of projects

----------Question- 3----------

Compared to traditional projects, the SAFe® portfolio enables

a) Decentralization of System Architecture.

b) More local empowerment for the teams.

c) Complete top-down control.

d) Good roles for the team members.

-------Answer-------

Correct answer is 'b.'

----------Question- 3----------

##

Levels

If SAFe® is implemented in an enterprise portfolio, the teams within that portfolio will be structured and identified with a set of levels. The team identified with a specific level has specific responsibilities and authority. By clearly specifying the expected responsibilities and authority of the teams at each level, SAFe® empowers them to be productive and collaborative so they can continuously move forward in their work. The identification of who needs to be at which level and what decision-making power they have enables the flow.

Fig. 4 summarizes these for 3-Level SAFe®. Each level provides a structure of work, roles, and activities. Notice how each level has a structure, a central responsibility, and authority (empowerment).

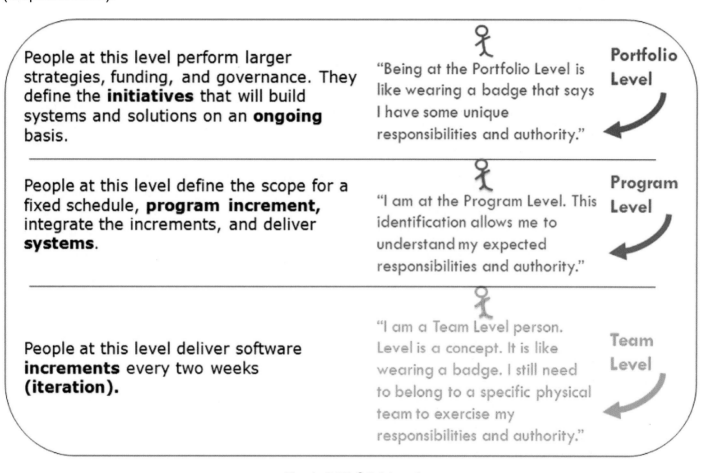

Fig. 4- SAFe® 3.0 Level

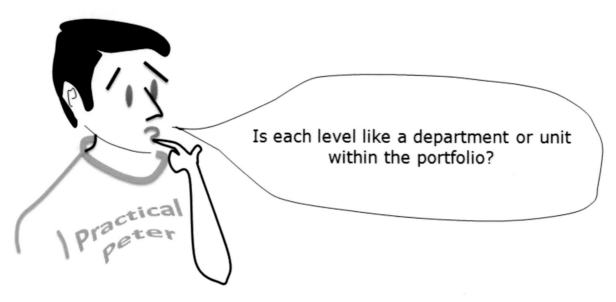

A level is not a department or unit. It is not physical but a concept. It simply says that a team at a certain level has a set of responsibilities and authority. A person in a level has kind of a virtual 'badge.' The badge offers the person a set of responsibilities and authority to facilitate and make decisions on specific content. For example, a business person in the Program Level can influence decisions on the product roadmap and what work is added to the Program Level Backlog. Still this is only a concept. The person has to part of a 'physical/tangible' team to really do anything. Fig. 5 shows the difference between the concept of 'Level' and the physical teams.

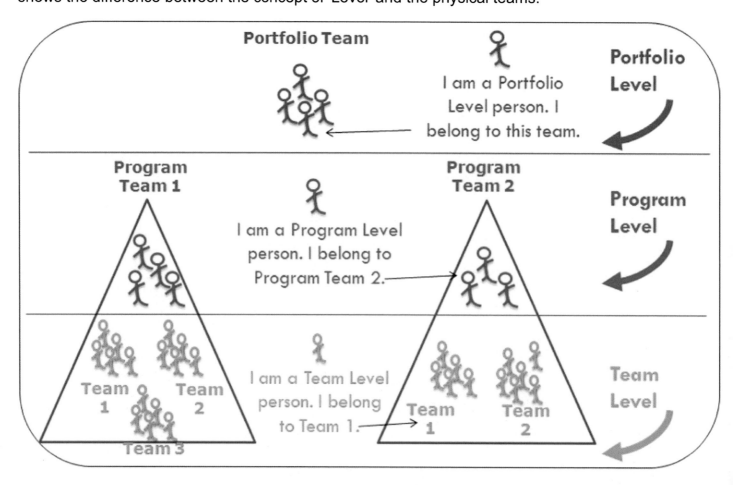

Fig. 5- A SAFe® Level is a concept

----------Question- 4----------

At the Program Level, _____ provides the strategic intent of the program, and _____ provides the scope for the next three program increments.

a) Work break down, Project plan.

b) Product Vision, Roadmap.

c) Milestones, Budget.

-------Answer-------

The Program Level is empowered to decide the Product Vision and the Roadmap. Correct answer is 'b.'

----------Question- 4----------

Scaled Agile upgraded SAFe® 3.0 to SAFe® 4.0 in 2016. In SAFe® 4.0, one more level, called the Value Stream Level, was added to scale the team for very large developments such as integrated hardware and software systems and firmware. So, most of the pure software development teams will not need this Value Stream Level.

People at this level define the scope in a fixed schedule (**program increment**), integrate the system increments, and deliver **solutions**. They are empowered for solution vision, roadmap, and local funding.

"I am at the Value Stream Level. This level is needed when large system of systems (solutions) are developed."

Portfolio Level

Value Stream Level

Program Level

Team Level

Fig. 6- SAFe® 4.0 Level

Going back to the bank example, Fig. 7 depicts the Deposit portfolio that has adopted 3-Level SAFe®. There is no Value Stream Level because the portfolio does not develop large solutions, or what is called a system of systems.

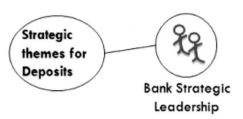

Fig. 7- SAFe® 3.0 Level for the Deposit portfolio

In SAFe®, the bank leadership defines the multi-year strategic themes for the Deposit portfolio. The Portfolio Team defines initiatives of 6 - 9 months duration in line with the strategic themes. Note that there can be multiple teams at the Program Level. Each team at the Program Level decomposes the initiatives related to their program to business features and plans how many features can be developed in 8 - 12 weeks. For example, the Savings Account Program Team decomposes the initiatives related to the Savings Account to business features. Finally, the teams at the Team Level decompose the business features into smaller business specifications and execute the two-week plan to build them. Such a clear separation of responsibilities and authority for each level enables the continuous collaboration and hence the flow of the work from the top (bank strategy) to the levels creating the value.

##

Discussion Scope

We now understand the outline of the SAFe® portfolio and the levels. As discussed in the Preface, this book is neither a comprehensive knowledge body of SAFe® nor does it explain the entire content of SAFe®. Instead, it purposefully spends most of the sections explaining the 'most common start-up approach of SAFe®' taken by many organizations. The focus of this start-up approach is to launch the Agile Release Train (ART). The rough sequence of the steps involved in launching the ART is shown in Fig. 8.

Launch ART

> Train everyone in SAFe®.
>
> Structure the Agile Teams.
>
> Group Agile Teams into the ART.
>
> Add support personnel (The Support).
>
> Bring the Agile Teams into synchronization and cadence (The Schedule).
>
> Groom the backlogs (The Scope).
>
> Perform the PI Planning (The Plan).

Work to meet the plan (The Execution).

Review the outcome. Step back, innovate, and retrospect. Prepare the next Plan (Cross the boundary).

Fig. 8- Discussion Scope - Partial

Training everyone involved in an ART is the first step to launching SAFe®. A summary of the training is discussed later in the Chapter 'Get the train moving.' The rest of the steps to launch the ART are discussed in dedicated chapters. The Chapter 'The Execution' explains how ARTs work within fixed time schedules after launching. Finally, the Chapter 'Cross the boundary' explains how the ART reviews the work, takes dedicated time to innovate and retrospect, and prepares for the next fixed schedule.

##

Agile Teams

SAFe® is distinctly identified by its positioning in an enterprise as a template for the portfolio. It is also distinct for the emphasis on the flow of value from the strategy to the customers. While these are distinguishing aspects of SAFe®, does SAFe® have anything in common with other Agile software development frameworks? SAFe®, like many other Agile frameworks, uses the Agile Team as its primary building block.

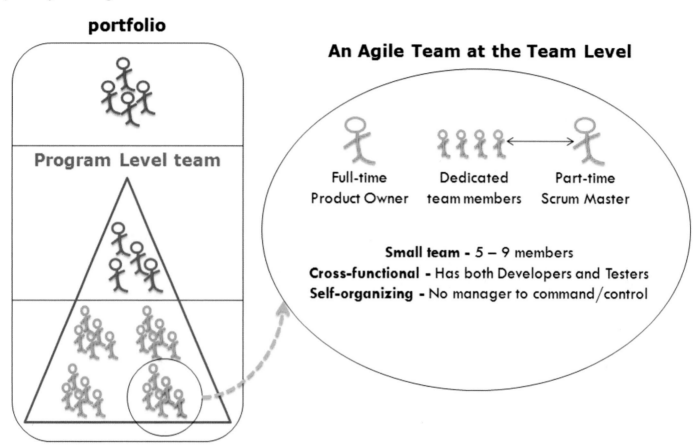

Fig. 9- Agile Team Structure

Each Agile Team has 5 – 9 members. The team members are fully dedicated to an Agile Team. Agile Teams are self-organized and not directed at the task level by someone like a project manager. Without a manager, the Agile Team plans and commits to the work. Agile Teams are also cross-functional having both Developers and Testers who work together towards common goals.

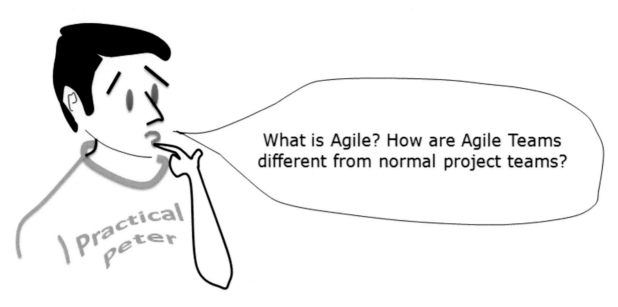

What is Agile? How are Agile Teams different from normal project teams?

Traditionally, many organizations use a development method called waterfall in their software projects. In waterfall projects, a detailed project plan is built that captures the details such as who has to do what activity, in what sequence, at what time, and within what duration to accomplish the project outcome. This plan is based on many assumptions and projections built on what is known today, which may be years before the software is actually released. After executing the complete plan, usually after a long time period, the software is delivered to users who will then provide feedback. If the feedback is positive and indicates the larger acceptance of the product, everyone is happy. However, such a happy ending is not always the case. Since the software was built using a big upfront long-term plan that was based on predictions and guesses for the most part, many things can turn out to be incorrect when released. For instance, the assumptions made about user behavior may be invalid. The interpretation of the project team about what the business people wanted may be incorrect. In addition, the external factors, market receptiveness, and assumptions might have changed. Sometimes the feedback may offer new insight that requires major modifications or the product itself may be identified as obsolete.

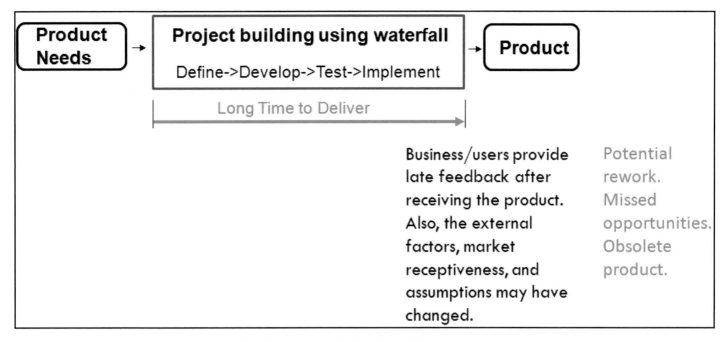

Fig. 10- Issues with Traditional Development

Concerned by the ineffectiveness of the waterfall planning approach to handle the dynamic nature of software development, a group of seventeen representatives of 'alternative implementations of software delivery models' gathered in 2001 in Utah to define a better way of creating software. This proclamation is called 'The Agile Manifesto' (agilemanifesto.org). The Agile Manifesto is a set of values and principles for a new way of software development. The Agile Manifesto, or simply 'Agile' as it is widely known, renounces the traditional waterfall-style big upfront long-term planning with a phase-gated process in favor of short iterative planning with **frequent software delivery in increments** for feedback. Agile places great importance on people interactions and employs **collaborative problem solving** to reach the iteration goals. Agile frameworks do not build detailed long-term project plans. Instead, they plan small iterations where a small amount of work is performed to create actual working software (the value). At the end of the iteration, the outcome is shared with the stakeholders and users for feedback. The insight from the feedback is used to plan the next iteration. Such an iterative and incremental approach gradually reduces the risks and increases value (useful software).

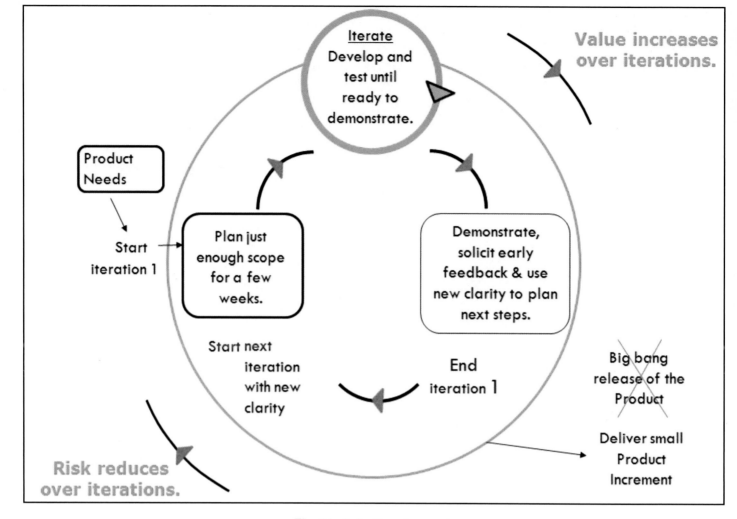

Fig. 11- Agile Development

----------Question- 5----------

In traditional methods of software development, the complete scope is finalized and locked down at the beginning of the project. This prevents the opportunity to

a)   Perform a daily stand-up meeting.

b)   Conduct frequent testing.

c)   Exploit the variability inherent in software development.

d)   Build better teams.

-------Answer-------

By deferring the refinement of work planned for the distant future until the actual time of development, the Agile Team creates the opportunity to respond to the emerging market conditions and even exploit any favorable conditions to deliver more value. Correct answer is 'c.'

----------Question- 5----------

Agile Teams are highly collaborative self-organizing teams. Self-organization means that without a manager the team members plan how to perform their work, execute the plan together, and track the progress against a common goal. They identify and resolve challenges together. One of the members of the Agile Team is the Product Owner. The Product Owner gets more value from the Agile Team by ensuring that the team works on product features having higher value first. The Product Owner is a dedicated individual who continually works with the team to help them understand the product needs and gets the best value out of their work. The Scrum Master is another role on the Agile Team. The Scrum Master is a part-time role played by a member of the Agile Team. In other words, the Scrum Master is a part-time Developer or Tester. The Scrum Master teaches and coaches Lean-Agile concepts and provides the status of the current work to management.

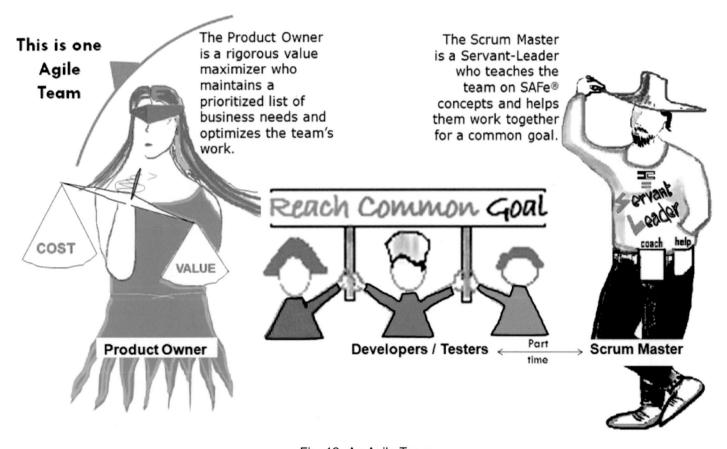

Fig. 12- An Agile Team

In summary, the building block of SAFe® is the Agile Team, but it does not work in isolation. Each Agile Team is always a part of a team of Agile Teams called the ART.

##

Agile Release Trains

SAFe® is distinctly identified by its positioning as a template for the enterprise portfolio and its emphasis on the flow of value from the strategy to the customers. Just like other Agile frameworks, SAFe® has the commonality of the Agile Team as its primary building block. How does SAFe® align the bottom-level Agile Teams to the Enterprise Level development strategies? How does SAFe® integrate the work of multiple Agile Teams when each team builds an individual part of a larger system? SAFe® uses a significant leverage called the Agile Release Train (ART) to integrate the work of multiple Agile Teams.

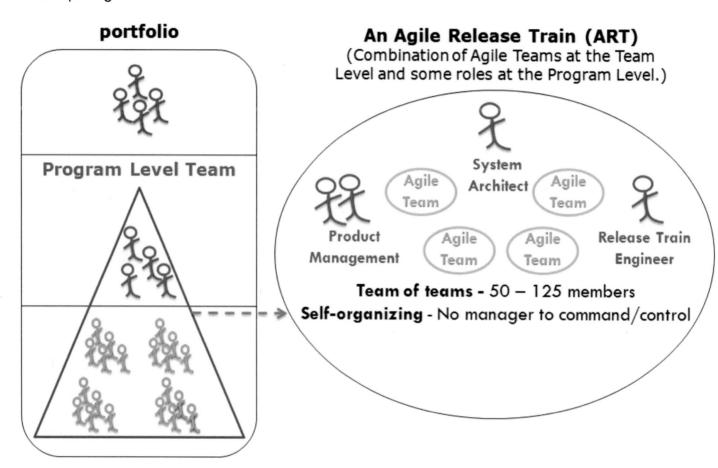

Fig. 13- ART Team Structure

In addition, the ART is leveraged for quickly launching SAFe® in an organization. The Chapter 'Get the train moving' explains this in detail.

----------Question- 6----------

An Agile Release Train consists of people from

    a)   The Program Level only.

    b)   The Team Level only.

    c)   Both the Program and Team Levels.

d) Multiple levels as preferred by the team.

-------Answer-------

There can be one or more ARTs in a portfolio. Each ART contains people from the Program and Team Levels. Correct answer is 'c.'

----------Question- 6----------

An ART is a long-lived team of 50 – 125 members. An ART comprises Agile Teams at the Team Level and a few additional roles at the Program Level. Just like the Agile Team, the ART is also a self-organized team. While an Agile Team defines the plan for a 2-week iteration, the ART, which is the collective group of the Agile Teams, defines the plan for 8 - 12 weeks (4 - 6 iterations).

Going back to the bank example, let us assume that each of the three product lines within the Deposit portfolio executes work which requires a permanent group of 50 - 125 people. The Deposit portfolio can consider forming three ARTs - Savings Account ART, Checking Account ART, and Long-Term Deposit ART. Now, it should be evident that a smaller number of people, less than 50, may not require an ART.

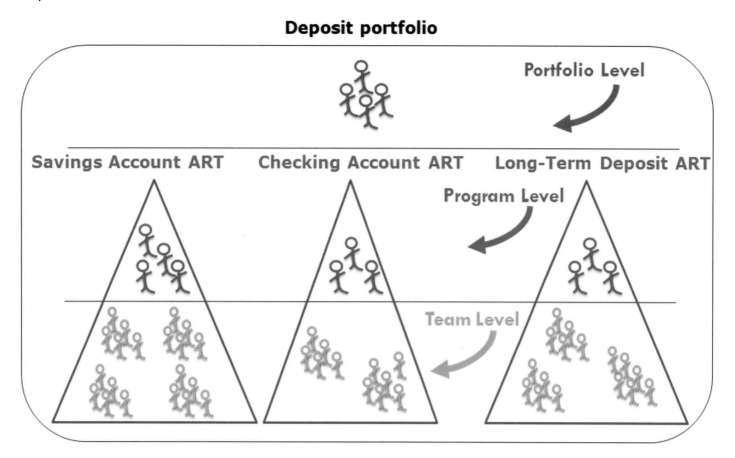

Fig. 14- ARTs in the Deposit portfolio

Product Management

Every ART has a Product Management role that provides the overall Program Level vision and the top business features for the upcoming Program Increment (PI), which has a duration of 8 - 12 weeks. The Product Management role can be one person or a group, but is usually a group of dedicated chief Product Managers and the Product Owners of all of the Agile Teams in the ART.

Release Train Engineer (RTE)

Every ART has a Release Train Engineer. The RTE is to the ART as the Scrum Master is to the Agile Team. The RTE is one individual who facilitates the activities of the ART. The RTE conducts the ART activity called the 'Scrum of Scrums' weekly or perhaps more often. The RTE and all the Scrum Masters of the Agile Teams participate in this event. The RTE or Product Management conducts another activity called the 'Product Owner (PO) Sync.' This is also weekly or more often and includes all of the Product Owners of the Agile Teams. Both the Scrum of Scrums and the PO Sync can be combined into a single meeting called the ART Sync. In all of these events, the participants discuss the cross-cutting concerns between the Agile Teams. Most of the time, the inter-team conflicts, new dependencies, risks, and the like will be the topics of discussion. The RTE facilitates the participants to help each other to meet common Program Level objectives.

System Architect

The System Architect facilitates the ART to meet the Non-Functional Requirements (NFR) of the business features. In addition, the System Architect collaborates with the teams and the Solution/Enterprise Architects in building the Architectural Runway. The Architectural Runway refers to the infrastructure code that is built ahead of the business functionality code. It ensures that enough technical infrastructure is in place to support the near-term business features.

Business Owner

Apart from these three roles, an appropriate executive from the Portfolio Level usually works with each ART. This executive has a good understanding of the enterprise strategies, the portfolio strategic themes, and the product vision. Sometimes this role may be played by a group of executives. This role is called the Business Owner. Every ART has a Business Owner who provides leadership for the overall vision and the proposed business features for the future work.

----------Question- 7----------

Which role facilitates most of the activities in the Program Level?

   a)   Scrum Master

   b)   Development Manager

c) Release Train Engineer

At the Program Level, the RTE facilitates the Lean-Agile way of working. Correct answer is 'c.'

----------Question- 7----------

In our company, we have project teams that are grouped into programs. So we already work as a team of teams. What is new with ART?

Practical peter

The teams of teams in traditional programs may not be long-lived teams but assembled for a specific duration. The teams of teams in SAFe® are long-lived. In the bank Deposit portfolio example, you saw that the ARTs were grouped around products. The reason is that a business product and its business operations are long-lived, and hence a software development team of teams formed around the product also lives as long as the product lives. Such longevity of the team provides several benefits such as enriching the domain, system, and process knowledge of the teams.

Another major difference is that the ART is a team of Agile Teams with a mutual understanding of common activities that happen at the same time (cadence). The teams integrate their plans, progress, and code (synchronization), which leads to intense collaboration, iteration after iteration.

----------Question- 8----------

Synchronization limits _____, while cadence makes wait times _____.

a) Predictability, variable

b) Variability, predictable

c) Complexity, lower

d) Predictability, reliable

To increase the predictability of the SAFe® events, ARTs follow a repeating pattern. For example, every 8 - 12 weeks ART level planning is done. If the Product Management wants to add a new opportunity but they missed the last planning event, they know that the train will arrive at the next planning event at the end of the current 8 - 12 weeks. This repeating pattern (cadence) makes wait times predictable. Cadence is inbuilt in many of the SAFe® activities. ARTs sync up, that is synchronize, the vision, plan, and working code at defined intervals. Such synchronization limits the variability between different people and their work. This is based on the SAFe® principle, "*Apply cadence, synchronize with cross-domain planning.*" Correct answer is 'b.'

----------Question- 8----------

##

The Schedule

SAFe® is a template for a way of working in enterprise portfolios. SAFe® accelerates the flow of value from the strategy to the customers. SAFe® uses the Agile Team as its primary building block. SAFe® leverages ARTs to scale and connect the Agile Teams. How do the ART and Agile Teams estimate and schedule their work?

As you recall SAFe® implements The Agile Manifesto, which renounces the traditional waterfall-style big upfront long-term planning with a phase-gated process in favor of short iterative planning with **frequent software delivery in increments** for feedback. Agile places great importance on people interactions and employs **collaborative problem solving** to reach the iteration goals. Agile frameworks do not build detailed long-term project plans. Instead, they plan small cycles (iterations) where a small amount of work is performed to create actual working software (the value). At the end of the iteration, the outcome is shared with the stakeholders and users for feedback. The insight from the feedback is used to plan the next iteration. Such an iterative and incremental cycle gradually reduces the risks and increases value (useful software). So, in effect each cycle is a learning opportunity to uncover the risks and discover the value.

Following the same approach, SAFe® does not create a detailed upfront plan or schedule. Instead SAFe® follows two learning cycles, one inside another. These learning cycles have fixed schedules (durations). The scope of the work is flexed to fit the schedules.

The ART keeps the outer cycle at a constant duration of 8 - 12 weeks. This outer cycle is called the Program Increment (PI). The PI starts after the PI Planning and ends with an Innovation and Planning (IP) iteration. In PI Planning, the ART selects the scope of what can be achieved in this fixed schedule (PI).

The inner cycle is called an iteration. Each iteration has a constant duration of 2 weeks. A PI will have 4 – 6 iterations (8 - 12 weeks) depending on the PI duration. Each iteration starts with Iteration Planning and ends with an Iteration Retrospective. In Iteration Planning, the Agile Team selects the scope of what can be achieved during that iteration. Within each iteration, there is development work and a Team Demo. Within one week of iteration completion, all of the ART Agile Teams integrate their work and preform an interim System Demo to the stakeholders. Development work continues while this integration occurs.

This inner cycle repeats until only one final iteration remains. The last iteration is called the IP iteration and is used to conduct the final PI Level System Demo.

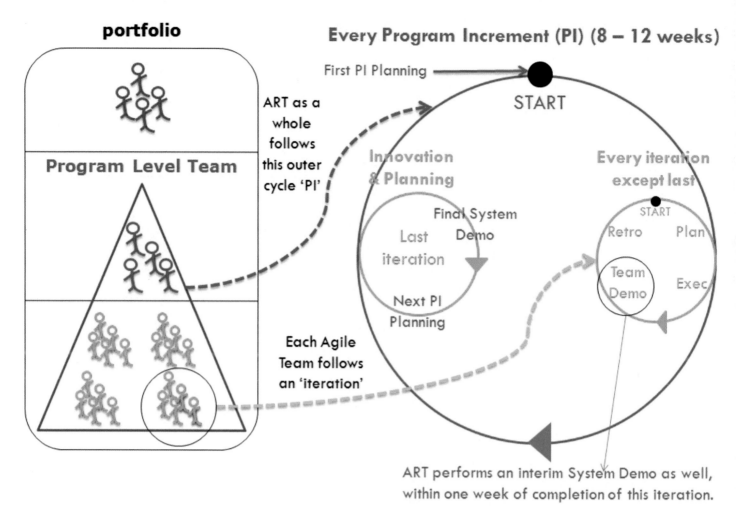

portfolio

Fig. 15- ART Schedule

----------Question- 9----------

A System Demo happens

   a)   When requested by the RTE.

   b)   Only at the end of a PI.

   c)   At the end of each iteration.

-------Answer-------

An interim System Demo happens within a week of the completion of each iteration. Correct answer is 'c.'

----------Question- 9----------

In summary, the outer cycle PI aggregates the work of all of the inner cycles (iterations). It forces all of the individual Agile Teams to integrate at least once per iteration. The teams learn from the feedback when they demonstrate their work (value) at the cycle boundaries – Iteration Demos (Inner

Cycle), and the interim System Demos, and the final PI Level System Demo (Outer Cycle). This is a brief overview of the process. More detail will be provided in the upcoming chapters.

Outer Cycle (PI)	Inner Cycle (Iteration)
Product Management provides the direction of what needs to be achieved in a PI.	The Product Owner collaboratively defines the goal for an iteration.
The ART (team of Agile Teams) delivers a system increment in the PI.	The Agile Team achieves an iteration goal in each iteration.
The final PI Level System Demo happens during the Innovation and Planning (IP) iteration.	The Team Demo happens within every iteration. The interim System Demo, which is the integration of the iteration work completed by all of the Agile Teams, happens within one week of each iteration completion, during the first week of the next iteration.

The cycles are not only time-boxed and repeating (cadence), but also serve to bring the stakeholders together at defined events (synchronization). Synchronization prompts the stakeholders to gain new insights and learn from them allowing the teams to incrementally improve the value. This is based on the SAFe® principle, "*Build incrementally with fast, integrated learning cycles.*"

----------Question- 10----------

Which activity implements cadence and synchronization between the Agile Teams in an ART?

a)   PI Planning

b)   Iteration Planning

c)   Project Planning

-------Answer-------

Correct answer is 'a.'

----------Question- 10----------

I get that. The Program Increment (PI) is roughly a schedule. It is basically every quarter. Does it mean that the PI is nothing but a Quarterly Release Schedule?

Practical Peter

PI is different from a Release in that a **PI is a time-box** to develop a system or solution increment while a **Release is a business event** that releases the system or solution increment to production. Within a PI, one or more Releases can be planned. This is based on the SAFe® objective "*Develop on Cadence, Release Any Time.*"

----------Question- 11----------

Is it mandatory to make production releases at the PI boundaries?

a)   Yes

b)   No

-------Answer-------

Production releases can be made anytime as per the business need. Correct answer is 'b.'

----------Question- 11----------

Going back to the bank example, Fig. 16 shows the contrast between the schedules done in waterfall and SAFe®.

Waterfall schedule of a large team with two sub teams that builds something for the Checking Account

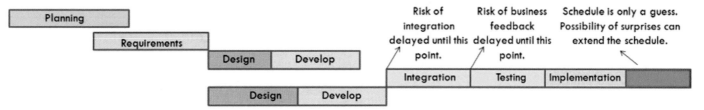

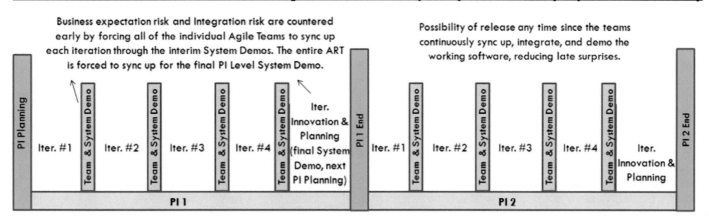

Fixed schedule of ART with a number of Agile Teams – Two cycles (PI & Iteration) repeat with certainty

Fig. 16- ART Schedule vs. Traditional Schedule

##

The Scope

Within an enterprise portfolio, SAFe® accelerates the flow of value from the strategy to the customers. Agile Teams build software (value). The ART, which is a long-lived team of Agile Teams, integrates and delivers the work of multiple Agile Teams. The ART works in a fixed time schedule called a PI, which is a learning cycle that repeats. How does the ART scope the work for the PI? How is the upcoming work captured?

In SAFe®, the upcoming work is organized as backlogs. Each backlog is a repository that captures the work to be performed for a specific team in each level. Each ART has a Program Backlog and each Agile Team has a Team Backlog.

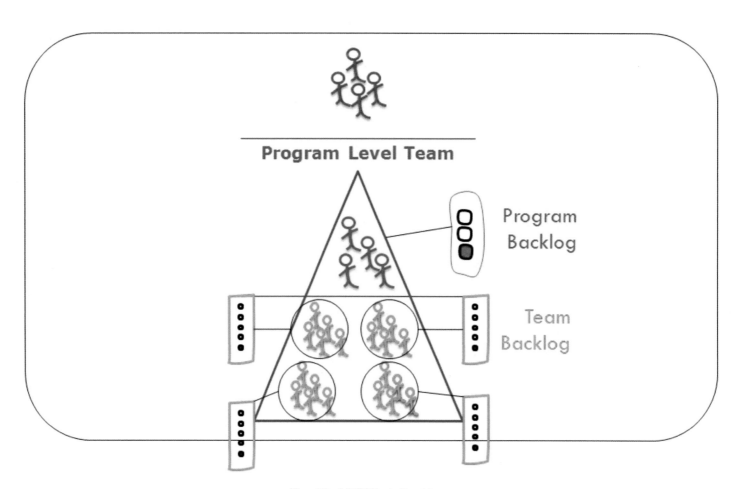

Fig. 17- ART Work Backlogs

Note the emphasis 'each team has a backlog.' Even if two teams are at the same level, each team has an individual backlog. The only commonality between the backlogs at the same level is that they all contain the same **type** of backlog items. For example, if there are two ARTs at the Program Level, there will be two Program Backlogs, both carrying a list of backlog items called **features**. Features are typical 'business features' like those used in normal marketing brochures. Team Backlogs contain backlog items called **stories**. A story captures the expected user value expressed in a simple statement. The statement format is similar to *'As a <User Role>, I would like <specific outcome> so that <expected benefit>.'* Stories can either be decomposed from a parent feature or locally identified by Agile Teams during the iterations.

Going back to the bank example, Fig. 18 shows the Program Backlog of the Savings Account ART and the Team Backlog of one of the Agile Teams.

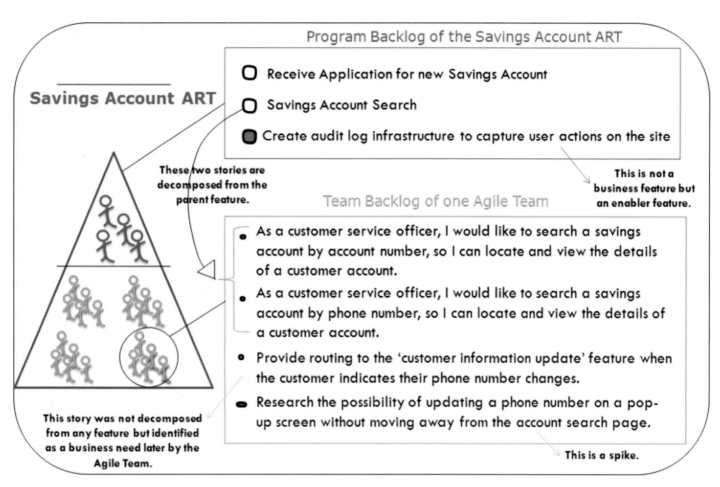

Fig. 18- Work Backlogs - Example

Enablers in the Backlogs

As one of the differentiators brought by SAFe®, work backlogs not only contain the business (functional) needs, but also reserve a portion of the backlog for technical needs. This is called **capacity allocation**. Capacity allocation ensures that the team invests in building the Architectural Runway, which is the infrastructure code to support the near-term business features. The backlog at every level captures the enablers. For example, the Enterprise Architect at the Portfolio Level defines *"enabler epics"* which are technology initiatives. Using the enabler epics, the Enterprise Architect provides strategic directions on technical concerns that cut across the portfolio such as technical stack, Portfolio Level infrastructure planning, hosting, etc.

A spike is a special type of enabler that is captured as a story in the Team Backlog.

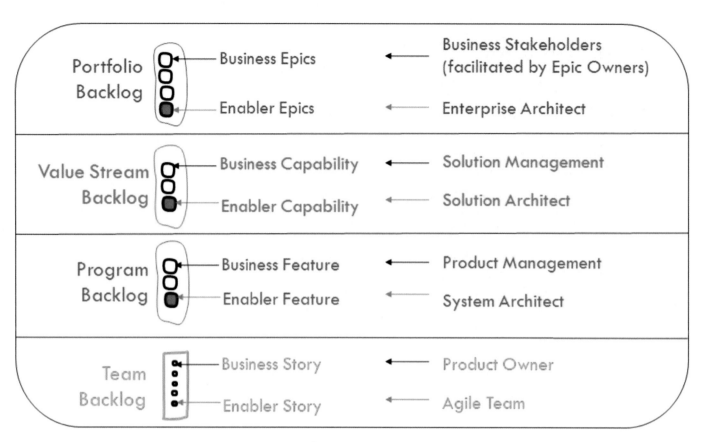

Fig. 19- SAFe® Work Backlogs – Enablers

Are the enablers the same as Non-Functional Requirements (NFR)?

Practical Peter

Well…there can be a relation. They are not the same however. An enabler is one of the work items in a backlog, whereas NFRs are the conditions applicable to the entire backlog. For example, 'Create the ability to log user actions on the site' can be an enabler (technical) feature. Just like any feature, it will have acceptance criteria, and the work is complete once the acceptance criteria are met. On the contrary, look at this example of an NFR, 'Every page on the site should have a response time of less than 3 seconds.' This NFR is applicable to each work item in the backlog to which this NFR is associated.

Usually, these NFRs are captured as part of the definition of done for the backlog. The definition of done refers to the conditions or constraints that the backlog items must meet in order to consider them completed (truly done). Each backlog must have a definition of done which in turn can contain NFRs. We mentioned that enablers and NFRs can have a relation. For instance, some of the NFRs start as enablers, are implemented, and then are added to the definition of done as NFRs. For example, the enabler 'Create a data mapping module to convert the input to XML format' can become an NFR later, 'All services should be able to accept input data in XML format.' Note that enablers resemble technical work, whereas NFRs resemble constraints.

----------Question- 12----------

What is true about a spike?

a)   A spike is a special name of a story that is reserved for capturing a Stretch Objective.

b)   A spike indicates a situation where a story during its development is found to be larger than the original estimate.

c)   A spike refers to a story that is planned for research or prototyping to learn more about something.

-------Answer-------

Spikes are learning stories. Usually, they are not meant to produce production code but to prove or disprove or learn about something. Correct answer is 'c.'

----------Question- 12----------

----------Question- 13----------

An ART has one single definition of done.

a) True

b) False

-------Answer-------

SAFe® recommends four types of definition of done that are scalable starting from the team stage to the release stage. They are

1. The definition of done for the Team Increment (used for the Team Demo).

2. The definition of done for the System Increment (used for the System Demo).

3. The definition of done for the Solution Increment (used for the Solution Demo).

4. The definition of done for the Release (used for the Production Release).

Correct answer is 'b.'

----------Question- 13----------

##

The Support

Within an enterprise portfolio, SAFe® accelerates the flow of value from the strategy to the customers. Agile Teams build software (value). The ART, which is a long-lived team of Agile Teams, integrates and delivers the work of multiple Agile Teams. The ART works in a fixed time schedule called a PI, which is a learning cycle that repeats. The ART and Agile Teams organize their work as Program Backlogs and Team Backlogs. The ART plans the scope of a PI by selecting features from the Program Backlog. The Agile Teams in the ART plan the scope of iterations by selecting stories from the Team Backlogs. So, the ART has a scope of work and a schedule to complete the scope. Can the ART and Agile Teams complete the scope by themselves?

The answer is that they may not. Typically in an enterprise, software development teams need the help of other teams to support the planning, designing, developing, testing, and deploying the software. So, in addition to the roles at the Program Level, SAFe® also offers a list of specialty roles for this support. The support roles are added as needed to the Program Level. In SAFe®'s "Big Picture," these roles are shown separately in a section called "Spanning Palette." Fig. 20 shows these additional specialty roles.

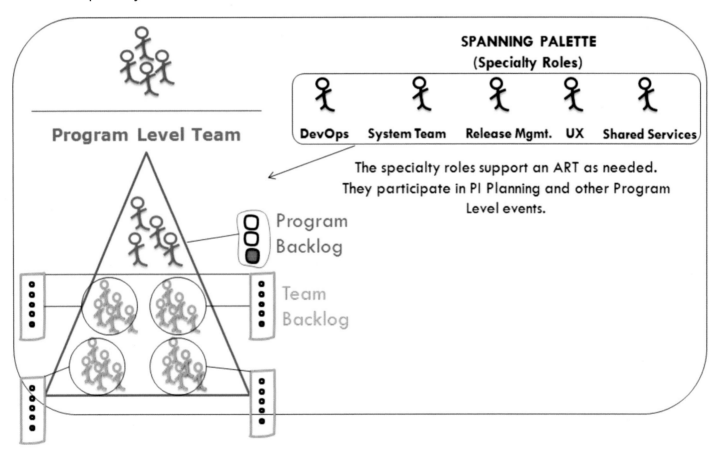

Fig. 20- Program Level – Specialty Roles

• DevOps – A set of practices such as integrating the IT operations personnel as part of the development teams, setting up the IT infrastructure for continuous deployment of ART deliverables, etc. to expedite the flow of team deliveries to actual use (production). The DevOps role helps the team to implement DevOps practices.

• System Team - It is a special Agile Team in the ART who helps all the other Agile Teams build the development infrastructure, setup the IT infrastructure for continuous integration of the work of the Agile Teams, and steward the System Demo.

• Release Management - A governance team that comprises those (usually the senior management in sales, marketing, quality, etc. in the organization) who have the knowledge of the business and IT operations, and external factors such as market conditions and regulatory compliance needs. They provide approval on release-related plans.

• Shared Services - Anyone who is available on a sharable basis but cannot be dedicated to a specific ART, such as Database analysts, System/Server Administrators, Trainers, etc.

• UX - UX is User Experience, a special knowledge area dealing with the design of digital user interfaces (for example- the web screen). An ART can have UX designers who will provide the overall vision and specific guidance for the UX of the system.

----------Question- 14----------

The "Spanning Palette" items can be considered for only the Program Level of SAFe®.

a) True.

b) False. They cannot be considered for any level.

c) False. They can also be considered for the Value Stream and Portfolio Levels.

-------Answer-------

The "Spanning Palette" can be considered for any of the three levels of SAFe®. For example, a group of interdependent ARTs can have a System Team (at the Value Stream Level) just like an ART (at the Program Level) can have a System Team. Correct answer is 'c.'

----------Question- 14----------

Is the Spanning Palette just a list of additional roles?

Practical Peter

No. The Spanning Palette not only defines the optional specialty roles but also the guidelines for bringing-in the associated specialty areas. For example, in addition to defining the role of DevOps personnel such as the Network Engineer, Database Administrator, etc., SAFe® also provides the process guidelines necessary for the DevOps culture and infrastructure. A similar process and design guideline is provided for the UX. Apart from the roles and guidelines for specialty disciplines, the Spanning Palette also defines the following items, which can be included by the teams if they are useful for their context.

- Vision - A long-term view of a portfolio, solution, or system.

- Roadmap - A near-term (usually six months) view of the team's deliverables. The Roadmap is used by the teams to provide a forecast to the stakeholders.

- Metrics - A list of optional metrics for each SAFe® level.

- Milestone - A specific point in time. It can be internal (PI milestones) or external (market event). A milestone, such as a PI end date (internal) or a regulatory compliance date (external), may influence the team's plan.

- Release - An event where the value (solution or system) is released for actual market use.

##

Get the train moving

SAFe® is best applied as a template for the enterprise portfolio. One of the top benefits of SAFe® is the acceleration of the flow of value from the strategy to the customers. Instead of a full-blown SAFe® transformation, that is- transitioning a complete portfolio into a SAFe® portfolio at the onset, it is common practice to quickly start with a simple ART when there are enough SAFe® constructs in place to start the work. If you review the build up of the SAFe® ART so far, notice that the ART resembles a fully assembled IT development program with a team, a work scope (backlogs), a schedule, support teams, and a business decision maker. It has enough constructs in place to start a development program that can deliver value.

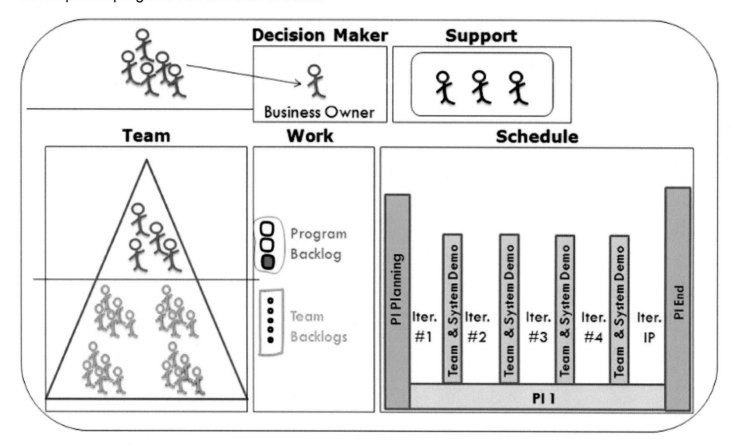

Fig. 21- An ART ready to start

An ART is not a full implementation of SAFe® however. It may not bring in all the good things SAFe® promotes including the **flow**. In spite of this, many organizations prefer to start with a simple ART to test the waters, review the outcome, and then start other ARTs. They may implement a full-blown SAFe® portfolio at a later date. Going back to the bank example, the Deposit portfolio may choose an implementation approach like Fig. 22. In this approach, the bank chooses to quickly launch a train Savings Account ART (1). Note there is no need for reorganizing anything outside this train including the Portfolio Level. Once the first train is launched, the bank has a plan to gradually launch the other trains (2 and 3). Finally, it plans to reorganize and structure the Deposit portfolio with a Portfolio Level

(4). The first train Savings Account ART will be launched using a SAFe®-recommended guideline called "*Implementing SAFe® 1-2-3.*" We will see more about this guideline in the next section.

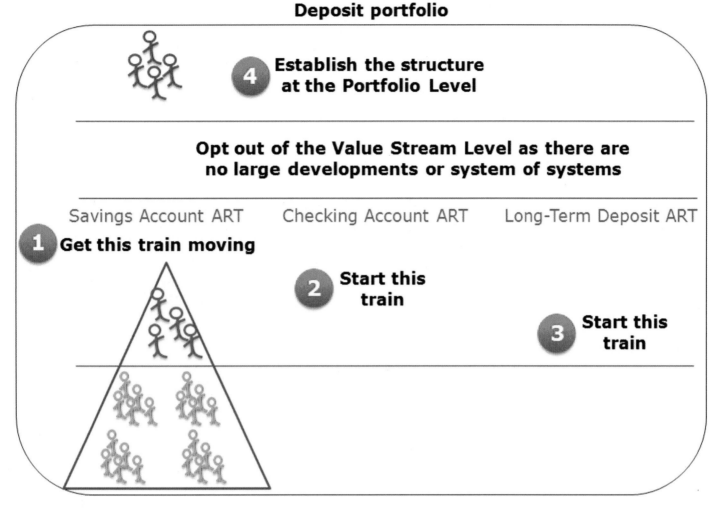

Fig. 22- Deposit Portfolio – SAFe® roadmap

Let us understand more about launching the train as recommended by SAFe®. Based on case studies of enterprises that went down the transformation path, Scaled Agile has abstracted one specific pattern as a guideline called "*Implementing SAFe® 1-2-3.*" This guideline consists of three steps.

1. Train Lean-Agile Change Agents – Change Agents are the starting point for a SAFe® transformation of an enterprise. If an enterprise forms a SAFe® transformation team, Change Agents will be its prominent members. They train and launch ARTs, and improve the ARTs using an "Inspect and Adapt" approach. For Change Agents, Scaled Agile offers a four-day training. After the training and upon passing a test, the Change Agents earn the certification "*SAFe® Program Consultant (SPC).*"

2. Train Lean-Agile Leaders – Lean-Agile Leader is not a role in SAFe® but refers to the management at different levels of an organization. While many Agile frameworks are not clear about how to engage the management, SAFe® takes an active approach to define management's behaviors

and responsibilities. Lean-Agile Leaders apply the Lean-Agile mindset and principles, coach the employees, unlock their intrinsic motivation, eliminate organizational level impediments for the teams, and facilitate change. SAFe® offers a two-day training for the leaders called "*Leading SAFe®*." After the training and upon passing a test, Lean-Agile Leaders earn the certification "*SAFe® Agilist (SA).*"

3. Train Teams and Launch the ART – A train can be launched, meaning they can start working on their first PI, in as little as a week through a training and immersion program called "*SAFe® QuickStart.*" In one week, Change Agents conduct a two-day training called "*SAFe® for Teams*" for all those in the ART. After the training, the participants get the certification "*SAFe® Practitioner (SP).*" This training is immediately followed by a two-day PI Planning session for the upcoming PI. PI Planning is where the ART and Agile Teams plan the scope for the upcoming PI. In the last day of this training week, orientation sessions are conducted for all the Scrum Masters and Product Owners in the ART. If desired, the Product Owners can take the two-day "*SAFe® Product Manager/Product Owner (SPMPO)*" training, and the Scrum Masters can take the two-day "*SAFe® Advanced Scrum Master (SASM)*" training.

----------Question- 15----------

Choose the correct statements. *"Implementing SAFe® 1-2-3"*

a) Is the standard Change Management Process for the SAFe® transformation.

b) Is based on hundreds of SAFe® implementation case studies.

c) Consists of three steps.

d) Is always implemented in one week.

-------Answer-------

SAFe® does not provide any standard Change Management Process for the SAFe® transformation. *"Implementing SAFe® 1-2-3"* is a guideline based on hundreds of SAFe® implementations and consists of three steps - Train Change Agents (1), Train Lean-Agile Leaders (2), and Train Teams and Launch the ART (3). While the third step can be launched using "SAFe® QuickStart" in one week, it is optional but not a requirement. Correct answers are 'b' and 'c.'

----------Question- 15----------

What specifically do the Change Agents and Lean-Agile Leaders do after they are certified?"

Practical Peter

Change Agents and Lean-Agile Leaders should not be confused with the specific SAFe® roles such as Product Management, RTE, etc.

The first step of a SAFe® implementation in an enterprise is the identification and training of its Change Agents. These internal Change Agents then train the organization's management (Lean-Agile Leaders) and the teams within the portfolio. They take the lead to launch the ART. Although there is no 'Coach' role in SAFe®, the Change Agents work is similar to coaching for a substantial amount of time in this initial period until an ART gets on its feet. Then they move onto the next ART. The Change Agents are critical enablers for the enterprise transformation into SAFe®.

SAFe® uses the term Lean-Agile Leaders to refer to the organization's management. It includes the traditional roles such as Development/Technical Managers, Directors, Division Heads, etc. Though SAFe® does not show these traditional roles in its "Big Picture," those roles still exist in SAFe®. The leaders in these roles continue to lead and groom their teams. They still allocate the budget to the teams. They work with their employees to setup career paths. They facilitate skill building and provide frequent feedback. By virtue of their experience and network, they mentor the teams to build relationships with customers, suppliers, etc. They work on the ground and help to remove the organizational hurdles that prevent the teams from making progress. It is common to see the managers along with the teams in the PI Planning. These roles are trained to exhibit Lean-Agile leadership behavior instead of traditional command and control. For example, the managers will mentor their teams to become self-organized so that the team can solve the day-to-day technical and team issues themselves rather than the managers owning or coordinating them. Another example is the managers will be on the ground interacting and observing the teams to understand the latest status rather than mandating the teams to create detailed daily status reports.

----------Question- 16----------

Intrinsic motivation refers to

a) Motivation using work environment.

b) Motivation using story telling.

c) Motivation using external recognition.

d) Motivation using incentives.

-------Answer-------

Lean-Agile Leaders motivate people by creating the right work environment. The work environment provides exciting challenges for the team. The challenges require the team to apply its best potential to solve problems. Such a work environment provides intrinsic motivation. External recognition and incentives can motivate temporarily but they are short-lived. Correct answer is 'a.'

----------Question- 16----------

##

Preparation for PI Planning

Launching the train requires that the trained Change Agents are in place, organization leaders involved with the ART are trained in Lean-Agile, and the ART members themselves are trained. In addition, many of following items need to be ensured, and they can happen right after the Change Agents' training.

•	Facilitate the Agile Teams within the ART to meet with each other and develop a mutual understanding. If there are existing Agile Teams, ensure that they are aligned so that they can start the PI together.

•	Remove the duplication or redundancy of development artifacts between the Agile Teams including the merging of code branches into a single branch.

•	Remove the duplication or redundancy of business artifacts between the Agile Teams including the merging of different product backlogs into a single backlog. Ensure that there is one Program Backlog with a minimum number of features.

•	Define the integration frequency between the Agile Teams.

•	Define a common definition of done for the System Demo.

•	Define the PI duration with specific start and end dates.

•	Ensure that the facilities and the logistics for the PI Planning are ready.

The trains are in motion once the PI Planning starts. For the first few PI Planning sessions, change agents may need to actively coach the RTEs in facilitating the PI Planning.

PI Planning is the central and most identifying event of SAFe®. This foundational event has a strong influence on all the subsequent activities in a PI. PI Planning enables the direct collaboration between visionaries and doers. PI Planning enables the explicit expression of issues, impediments, risks, and the resolutions by having all the stakeholders and decisions-makers together in literally the same room. PI Planning brings cadence (the alignment of events to start, frequently meet, and end at the same time) to the different teams so that it reduces their collaboration complexity. PI Planning enables synchronization (coming together to reduce differences) between different teams so that it reduces integration surprises. Keeping these factors in mind, PI Planning events are diligently prepared for full effectiveness. In general, preparations in the following three areas are ensured.

• Are the teams staffed and critical roles like the RTE, Scrum Masters, and Product Owners assigned? Is there alignment between the business stakeholders on the business priorities?

• Are the current business context and the Program Backlog with top business features, technical features (enablers), and constraints (NFRs) available?

• Is there logistics support such as a large room for the ART gathering available and additional breakout rooms for the individual Agile Teams to plan?

----------Question- 17----------

Preparation for the PI Planning is required only when

a) Executives participate.

b) The number of the participants goes beyond a threshold.

c) Multiple ARTs need to work together.

d) None of the above.

-------Answer-------

PI Planning is a significant event where all the ART members including the business executives and the specialty roles participate. It always requires careful preparation. Correct answer is 'd.'

----------Question- 17----------

##

The Plan

Within an enterprise portfolio, SAFe® accelerates the flow of value from the strategy to the end users. Even before the portfolio is completely transitioned into a SAFe® portfolio, organizations can readily start SAFe® with just one ART. The ART is a long-lived team of Agile Teams that integrates and delivers the work of multiple Agile Teams. The ART works in a fixed and repeating time schedule called a PI. The ART flexes the scope of work to match the schedule. When does the ART finalize the scope and plan for the PI? Just at the boundary of the current PI, the ART plans for the next PI in an event called PI Planning. PI Planning is a foundational event conducted over one and a half to two days. It brings all the people in an ART together to understand the context of business problems and solution vision. It facilitates the ART to finalize the plans for the upcoming PI by understanding, deliberating, and synchronizing the interfacing/cross-cutting issues.

Literally everyone in an ART from the senior business executive to the junior team member participates in this event. Fig. 23 shows a simple PI Planning agenda for an ART.

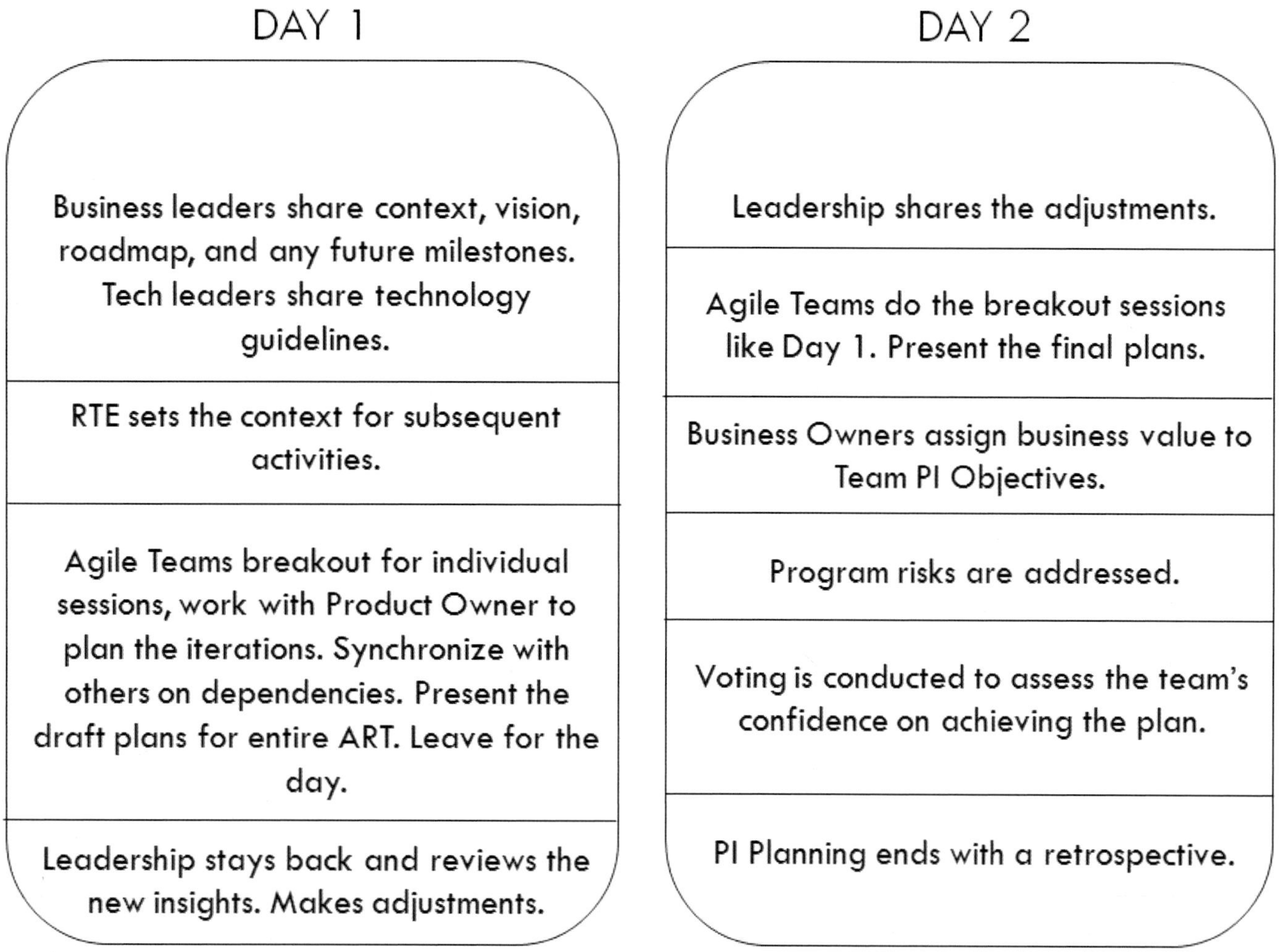

DAY 1

Business leaders share context, vision, roadmap, and any future milestones. Tech leaders share technology guidelines.

RTE sets the context for subsequent activities.

Agile Teams breakout for individual sessions, work with Product Owner to plan the iterations. Synchronize with others on dependencies. Present the draft plans for entire ART. Leave for the day.

Leadership stays back and reviews the new insights. Makes adjustments.

DAY 2

Leadership shares the adjustments.

Agile Teams do the breakout sessions like Day 1. Present the final plans.

Business Owners assign business value to Team PI Objectives.

Program risks are addressed.

Voting is conducted to assess the team's confidence on achieving the plan.

PI Planning ends with a retrospective.

Fig. 23- PI Planning - Agenda

Here is the narration of the PI Planning events.

Day One

• PI Planning starts with the context setting by the Business Owner about the overall vision, proposed features for this PI, and any near-term roadmap.

• Product Management re-emphasizes the overall vision and presents the top features for the PI.

• System Architects and any Technical/Development Managers, who are called "*Lean-Agile Leaders*" in SAFe®, present guidance on the Architecture and Development practices to be followed during the PI.

• Product Management hands over a separate set of features to the respective Product Owner of each Agile Team. At this point, each Agile Team breaks out to a separate location. The locations are not too remote but are within earshot of each team.

• Each Agile Team decomposes the features into stories with the help of the Product Owner. Each team identifies the dependencies with other teams and negotiates mutual plans to sequence the work as appropriate to address the dependencies. Each Agile Team also identifies any technical spike (enabler story) that may need addressing. All the stories are estimated using techniques like Planning Poker. Each Agile Team calculates its capacity (how much work it can do per iteration) by assuming an initial productivity (velocity) of 8 story points per team member.

• All Agile Teams capture the risks that constantly emerge from the planning process. The RTE separately conducts the Scrum of Scrums where the Scrum Masters check-in every 45 minutes. If they find a need to discuss any focused issues, the affected Scrum Masters get together in a Meet-after session.

• The last iteration of a PI is called an IP iteration in which the ART takes up innovation activities and performs the next PI Planning. For example, in a PI with five iterations, no stories are planned for the fifth iteration, which will be the IP iteration. In iterations one to four, each Agile Team plans how many stories it can complete.

• The Agile Team usually uses a board (something like a white board) to capture the plan. The board is divided into sections for each of the four iterations. The board also has a section for Team PI Objectives, a section for Stretch Objectives, and a section for dependencies/risks.

• Each Agile Team summarizes the business problems that will be solved in the upcoming PI in terms of one or more PI Objectives. These four elements – iterations with their stories, PI Objectives, Stretch Objectives, and the dependencies/risks - are broadcasted publicly through their board to the rest of the ART members. When each Agile Team is required to present its plan later, the team will use this board as a reference.

- Separately, the RTE facilitates the ART to capture the Program Level dependencies on a program board. The program board broadcasts the cross-cutting dependencies between all of the Agile Teams.

- During Day One, the teams strive to get one full pass of all iterations and arrive at PI objectives rather than a detailed and accurate plan. By the end of Day One, the Agile Teams present their draft plans (captured on their board) to the key ART stakeholders in the presence of other ART members.

- Many of the ART members leave for the day while the key ART stakeholders (ART Program Level Team, Scrum Masters, Product Owners) remain. These stakeholders review the plans. Based on the new insights, they identify any adjustments required to the team composition and scope.

----------Question- 18----------

What captures the forecast of expected releases in the next three PIs?

a) Vision

b) Roadmap

c) Backlog

-------Answer-------

The roadmap captures the expected market releases for the next three PIs. Correct answer is 'b.'

----------Question- 18----------

Day Two

Just like on Day One, everyone in the ART from the senior business executive to the junior team member participates.

- Day Two begins with the ART leadership presenting any adjustments to the scope, team composition, and any other elements to the ART.

- The Agile Teams once again breakout for refinement to their plan based on the new adjustments.

- The RTE keeps updating the program board with the emerging dependencies between the features.

- The Agile Teams present their final plans.

- The Business Owner assigns a relative value to each of the PI Objectives. This value provides an idea of the business importance and aligns the team with the business priorities.

- Each Program Level risk is addressed through one of these means - Resolved-Owned-Accepted-Mitigated. This approach is known as ROAM.

- After the plans are finalized, the RTE asks the team to express their confidence level of meeting this plan. The team does this by raising their fingers on a scale of one to five. All five fingers raised- indicates the highest confidence on delivering the PI Objectives. Team members with lower confidence are encouraged to share their concerns, and actions are taken to address those concerns.

- PI Planning comes to an end with each Agile Team committing to a set of PI Objectives and their Team Backlog. The Team PI Objectives are rolled into the Program PI Objectives.

- All Agile Teams within an ART have a common vision, roadmap, Program Backlog, and set of Program PI Objectives. They also have individual Team Backlogs and Team PI Objectives.

----------Question- 19----------

What are the correct statements about PI Planning?

a) PI Planning is where epics are reviewed and approved by the Program Portfolio Management.

b) A demonstrable solution or system is created in PI Planning.

c) PI Planning happens at the beginning of an iteration.

d) The ART comes together to understand the Program PI Objectives.

e) PI Planning is facilitated by the Scrum Master.

f) Multiple ARTs collaborate together to plan their upcoming PI.

g) The ART works together to plan and flush out risks and dependencies.

-------Answer-------

PI Planning for the upcoming PI happens at the boundary of the current PI. PI Planning is the most critical part of the SAFe® execution where all stakeholders of an ART come together to understand the Program PI Objectives, flush out risks and dependencies, and commit to individual Team Level PI Objectives. Correct answers are 'd' and 'g.'

----------Question- 19----------

Hold on! I have never heard of things like PI Objectives and Stretch Objectives. Are they different from Program Backlog features?

PI Objective

The Team PI Objectives are short statements of business or technical outcome in plain language. Although they are mostly about end-user functionality, they can also be milestones, research initiatives, etc. These objectives are created by the teams with the Product Owner's help. Team PI Objectives are crafted using the guidelines of SMART (Specific, Measurable, Achievable, Realistic, Time-bound).

Team PI Objectives are different from features in that PI Objectives are exclusive goals committed to by an individual Agile Team while a feature may span multiple Agile Teams. PI Objectives prompt the team to understand and commit to business outcomes while providing visibility of their plan to the business. The Business Owner assigns an expected business value to each Team PI Objective after interacting with the Agile Team to understand them. This value-assigning exercise makes the business intent transparent. Later, during the IP iteration, the Business Owner assigns an actual business value to indicate how much value was actually realized. The ratio between these two scores, the original value and the actual value, is used to calculate the Program Predictability Measure. This measure is one of the SAFe® metrics and helps the stakeholders to understand the dynamics of the associated ART.

----------Question- 20----------

Which measure is an aggregate of Team PI Performance Reports of all the teams in an ART?

a) Epic Progress Measure

b) Value Stream Predictability Measure

c) Program Predictability Measure

d) PI Burn-down chart

The Team PI Performance is the ratio between the actual business value vs. the expected business value of the Team PI Objective of an Agile Team. The aggregate of the Team PI Performance of all the Agile Teams in an ART is called the Program Predictability Measure. A measurement of 80% or above is regarded as sufficient to run the business. Correct answer is 'c.'

----------Question- 20----------

----------Question- 21----------

Select the true statements.

a)   The Team PI Objective is provided by the Business Owner.

b)   By assigning values to the Team PI Objectives, the Business Owner clarifies the business priorities and helps the team to align with these priorities.

c)   The Team PI Objective is a collection of features.

d)   The Team PI Objective is an abstraction of the team goal for the PI.

-------Answer-------

Correct answers are 'b' and 'd.'

----------Question- 21----------

Stretch Objective

Each Agile Team can also create Stretch Objectives. A Stretch objective indicates additional work that may be taken up by the Agile Team if it completes the committed PI Objectives and has more capacity. Stretch Objectives also help create a capacity margin that can be used for handling uncertainties that may emerge around the committed objectives. Typically 10 - 15% of the team capacity is set aside for Stretch Objectives.

----------Question- 22----------

At the end of PI Planning, the ART produces Program PI Objectives and a program board. Which one explicitly depicts the dependencies between team features?

a)   Program PI Objectives

b)   Program board

c)   Both

d)   None

  -------Answer-------

Correct answer is 'b.'

----------Question- 22----------

                                                        ##

The Execution

After PI Planning, each Agile Team starts the first iteration. An iteration is two weeks in duration where all of the Agile Teams in an ART produce an integrated and tested deliverable for the interim System Demo.

Base Practice and Complementary Practice

An Agile Team can follow either ScrumXP or Team Kanban practices as needed to define, build, test, and integrate their work. The choice of what to use as a base practice – ScrumXP or Team Kanban is decided by the nature of the work. If the work requires short-term planning and the team will not be interrupted with changes in between (short-term commitment of scope), ScrumXP is chosen as the base practice, and Kanban is leveraged as a complementary practice to visualize the work and improve the flow. If the work is unpredictable and the priorities shift daily (no commitment of short-term scope), Kanban is chosen as the base practice, and the ScrumXP practices like the Daily Standup, Continuous Integration, etc. are leveraged for work efficiency. Throughout the PI, the Agile Team can seek the help of others at the Program Level like the System Architect, System Team, DevOps, Shared Services, etc. as required.

Inner Cycle - The Iteration

Each iteration starts with Iteration Planning where the team works with the Product Owner and commits to an iteration goal. The stories required to accomplish the iteration goal are selected into the iteration. Most of the time, these stories have already been identified during the PI Planning. If that is the case, the team works on elaborating the stories into tasks. Then it builds and tests the stories. Towards the end of the iteration, the team performs the Team Demo where the tested feature is demonstrated to the Product Owner and the stakeholders. Then the Agile Team holds an Iteration Retrospective to identify any potential improvements in their way of working. Within a week from the completion of the iteration, the Agile Team performs the interim System Demo, which is the demonstration of the integrated work of all the Agile Teams within an ART.

This cycle – Plan, Define, Execute, Test, Demo, and Retrospect – is repeated for all of the iterations except the last one. In the last iteration called the *"IP Iteration,"* the ART conducts a final fully integrated demo called the *"PI System Demo"* to the stakeholders.

SAFe® uses the principle *"Unlock the intrinsic motivation of knowledge workers"* so that the Agile Teams can bring up the ground-level intelligence (bottom-up intelligence) needed to perform their job better. By self-organizing their work, they ensure the continuous flow of valuable work without waiting for any external guidance or decision on every single issue.

----------Question- 23----------

An Agile Team takes up a story and completes the related tasks one by one in a sequence. This approach is called

a) Waterfalling the iteration.

b) Team Kanban.

c) Scrum.

-------Answer-------

Decomposing the stories into tasks and completing them in parallel is the more effective approach. Working on the tasks serially is called waterfalling the iteration. Correct answer is 'a.'

----------Question- 23----------

Systems or software building is a knowledge (not physical labor) driven work where the people closer to the work often have more knowledge and local information about the work than their bosses. So it is important for the bosses (managers) to empower their ground-level team members to collectively decide how to perform and troubleshoot the work without any external direction. Allowing these members to make decisions subject to certain decision-making guidelines expedites timely and relevant decisions. In addition to these benefits, providing opportunities to the ground-level teams to solve the problems on their own increases their motivation and commitment towards the job.

"Built-In Quality" from the Beginning

A challenge for new Agile Teams is how to build quality increments in fast-paced two-week iterations. One of SAFe®'s four core values is "*Built-in Quality*." SAFe® advocates that Agile Teams build the quality from the beginning to reap the following benefits: Customer satisfaction; Predictability and integrity; Scalability; Velocity, agility, and system performance; and Innovation. During the initial days, this is where the Agile Teams need more coaching.

In particular, Agile Teams need to be competent in Extreme Programming (XP) because they need the XP practices of Continuous Integration, Test-First, Refactoring, Pair Work, and Collective Code Ownership to build the quality from the beginning. The teams merge the code multiple times a day and maintain a single main branch. While local integrations are performed daily, full system integration is done at least once or twice per iteration. This ensures that the differences between the teams are minimized. The teams also apply Test-Driven Development (TDD), where an automated unit test is written and then code is written to pass that test (traditionally it is the other way around), or Acceptance Test-Driven Development (ATDD), where an automated acceptance test is written first before the code. This ensures the availability of tests for regression testing as the system evolves. Through refactoring, the teams restructure the code continuously in a series of small steps without altering the external code behavior. This allows the teams to keep the code in maintainable condition. The teams follow Pair Work on coding, testing, reviewing, and integrating. Pair Work increases the chance of building quality in from the beginning while helping with refactoring, maintaining standards, and increased automation.

Oops. There seems to be a lot to learn for Agile Teams. Can they do it?

Practical Peter

Yes, Agile Teams need to learn many things. They need focused mentoring to become good in applying Lean-Agile practices. SAFe® has some elements that facilitate this learning. First is the role of the Scrum Master. The second and third learning enablers are IP iterations and Communities of Practice (CoP).

Scrum Master is a Servant-Leader of the Agile Team who teaches the team to learn and follow ScrumXP practices. In organizations new to Agile, it is hard to get competent Scrum Masters. In such cases, it might be essential to hire Scrum Masters with experience of Scrum, XP, and Kanban for the initial period.

IP iteration is the last iteration of a PI. Stories are not planned for this iteration. The IP iteration is intentionally kept as a time to break away from the monotonous delivery-based thinking of the previous iterations and drive innovation and learning-oriented activities. This iteration can be used by the team to conduct learning exercises and experimentations, install and fine-tune development infrastructure, support any production releases, etc.

Communities of Practice (CoP) are interest groups formed outside the ARTs. CoPs allow the team members in a portfolio to form a focused group around a subject matter, share the knowledge, and groom their skills. For example, there can be a CoP on XP practice of Test-Driven Development. There can be another on Scrum. There are no limits. The Scrum Master takes an active role in identifying the gaps and encouraging the team members to be part of the appropriate CoPs.

----------Question- 24----------

During the execution, the Agile Team does NOT spend any time with others in the ART and focuses only on their iteration work.

a)   True

b)   False

-------Answer-------

The Agile Team does focus a lot on their iteration progress. It builds the stories in parallel and tracks the progress using Kanban boards. However, the Agile Team also collaborates with other teams to create an integrated increment for the interim System Demo. The Agile Team members often work with the ART team members such as the System Architect as needed throughout the iteration. Correct answer is 'b.'

----------Question- 24----------

One of SAFe®'s four core values is *"Built-in Quality."* What are the other three values?

SAFe® values are a set of beliefs. These values create the desired results from the SAFe® implementation. There are four values: Alignment, Built-in Quality, Transparency, and Program Execution. Here is a summary of what each value means.

SAFe® Values

1. Alignment

Alignment of the teams at every level to the enterprise strategic objectives.

Implementation: Traceability of top-level enterprise objectives to the stories at the bottom (Team Level) through Kanban. Clear lines of leadership and delegation across the layers.

2. Built-in Quality

Quality will not be deferred until later. It is injected from the beginning.

Implementation: Emphasis on using solid engineering practices from Extreme Programming (XP) during the iteration that help to build quality from the beginning.

3. Transparency

Continuous visibility of the work pipeline (backlogs), current work status, and the outcome.

Implementation: Visibility of the work pipeline through Kanban. Visibility of progress through demos at the iteration and PI boundaries.

4. Program Execution

Convert the plan into an implementation to achieve the outcome.

Implementation: Get the work engine moving by launching the ART as soon as possible. Gradually scale up the execution to the next levels.

##

Cross the boundary

Time to Step Back

The last iteration of the PI is called the Innovation and Planning (IP) iteration. In all of the other iterations, the ART focuses on development to achieve the Program PI Objectives. The IP iteration is the time to step back and shift from '**development**' mode to '**learning and improving**' mode. Some of the specific events planned in this iteration are

•   Completion of any remaining development activities related to the current Program PI Objectives for the final integration and release. A full system integration must happen here if it has not occurred in prior iterations. It is mandatory to have at least one full integration in a PI.

•   An Inspect and Adapt workshop that facilitates the PI System Demo and ART Retrospective.

•   Research and improvement activities.

•   Backlog grooming and PI Planning for the next PI.

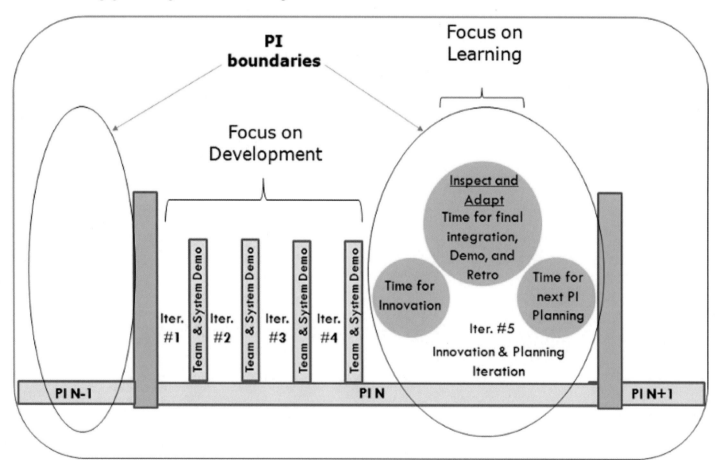

Fig. 24- PI Boundaries

IP Iteration as a "Guard Band"

The IP iteration is intentionally kept as a break from the monotonous delivery-based thinking of the previous iterations. Instead it drives innovation and learning-oriented activities. In addition to providing time for retrospection and research, the IP iteration also serves as a *"guard band,"* or estimating buffer, for the ART. Stories are not planned for these last two weeks, which prevents 100% utilization of the team, but this additional time (buffer) guards the PI against any surprise work that emerges during the development and threatens the time-box (schedule). Note that the Team Velocity is only calculated for the development iterations and not for the IP Iteration.

ART performs Inspect and Adapt workshop

The final PI System Demo and Retrospective happen in the Inspect and Adapt workshop. Unlike the traditional phase-gated software development models where the completion of a phase is considered a milestone, the PI System Demo is the moment of truth for the ART to objectively evaluate if they really created value. The progress is acknowledged by demonstrating the working system to the stakeholders. This is based on the SAFe® principle, "*Base milestones on objective evaluation of working systems.*"

While a local retrospective is performed by every Agile Team, the Retrospective that occurs in the Inspect and Adapt workshop is larger in scope and simultaneously performed by the ART as a single team. The potential improvements are captured as stories and taken to the next PI Planning. The team can review everything that influenced their way of working such as the working environment, development infrastructure, etc.

The Inspect and Adapt workshop can happen at any point during the IP iteration as long as there is enough time afterwards for the PI Planning.

ART experiments, innovates, and learns

The majority of the IP iteration time is reserved for non-development activities such as hackathons, innovation games, and improvements through which the ART is refreshed and recharged. Assuming that the ART has no leftover work from development when it enters the IP iteration, it may use one half to a full day for the Inspect and Adapt workshop and one and a half to two days for the PI Planning for the next IP. That leaves plenty of time in these two weeks for learning activities. CoPs actively promote small innovation efforts, contests, and learning experiments. Some teams conduct business-IT innovation and prototype sessions. Even the individual team members can investigate their own areas of interest as long as they are related to the strategies and mission of the organization. These non-development activities can occur at any time during the IP iteration.

Release Management periodically reviews and approves the Release

Release Management conducts Release Management Review meetings weekly or more frequently as needed. They provide approval on release-related plans. The Release can happen anytime during the PI, subject to business needs. In practice, many ARTs plan formal Releases during the IP iteration to take advantage of the increased time and support available for the release processes. Release Management is an optional support role defined in the SAFe® "*Spanning Palette.*" An exclusive role for Release Management can be defined depending on the governance needs for the releases.

Planning for the next PI

The ART performs the PI Planning for the next PI in the IP iteration. PI Planning must occur after the Inspect and Adapt workshop, but there are no other stipulations for when it must occur.

PI comes to an end and the next PI begins

When the last iteration – IP iteration – is over, the PI comes to an end. This cycle – Development and Integration by the Agile Team through iterations, Crossing the boundary through the IP iteration – is repeated for the next PI.

----------Question- 25----------

The IP iteration is the only opportunity to integrate the work of all the Agile Teams.

a) True

b) False

-------Answer-------

The Agile Teams integrate their work within one week of every iteration end. The only exception where the teams need to wait until the IP iteration is when there is a large development involving solutions (systems of systems). Such large solution developments usually need special arrangements like additional devices and hardware, and these are not practical in every iteration. Correct answer is 'b.'

----------Question- 25----------

##

Check on the Discussion Scope

The primary scope of this book is to explain the most common start-up approach to SAFe® - launching the ARTs. You now understand the ART and its structure, Change Agents, training, fixed PI schedule, PI Planning, Program PI Objectives (scope), execution, and how to cross over to the next PI. Now we need to understand the rest of the components that make up the full SAFe® portfolio. Fig. 25 shows what we have covered so far and what comes next.

Launch ART

> Train everyone in SAFe®.
>
> Structure the Agile Teams.
>
> Group Agile Teams into the ART.
>
> Add support personnel (The Support).
>
> Bring the Agile Teams into synchronization and cadence (The Schedule).
>
> Groom the backlogs (The Scope).
>
> Perform the PI Planning (The Plan).

Work to meet the plan (The Execution).

Review the outcome. Step back, innovate, and retrospect. Prepare the next Plan (Cross the boundary).

Scale up the ARTs (Value Streams).

Expedite the value flow from the top (The Portfolio).

Fig. 25- Discussion Scope

##

Value Streams

We understand that enterprises can readily start SAFe® with just one ART. An ART scales small Agile Teams (5 - 9 members) into a large team (50 – 125 members). Now, what if the enterprise needs to have more than 125 team members and all of them need to work together (interdependent) to produce a single solution? We may need to have more ARTs and an approach to integrate their work.

In the bank example, we saw that the bank had three ARTs in the Deposit portfolio. Those three ARTs were fairly independent. Let us say that the bank has acquired another bank which offers only a savings product. For strategic reasons, it was decided that the savings products of the two banks will not be integrated at the system level, and they will continue as two separate divisions. The bank leaders also want to provide a unified experience for every savings product-related transaction irrespective of which division is chosen by the bank's customer. The following is what occurred. The team that supports the acquired bank's savings account is structured to work as a new ART. So there are two savings ARTs now- Core Savings ART and New Savings ART. Since the bank wants to build a unified experience and mutually leverage each other's features, these two ARTs need to closely coordinate their product vision, roadmap, development, and maintenance. How can the bank coordinate the dependencies between these two ARTs? This is where it might make sense to scale up to the next level of SAFe® – the Value Stream Level. The bank Deposit portfolio did just that. A Value Stream Team was added.

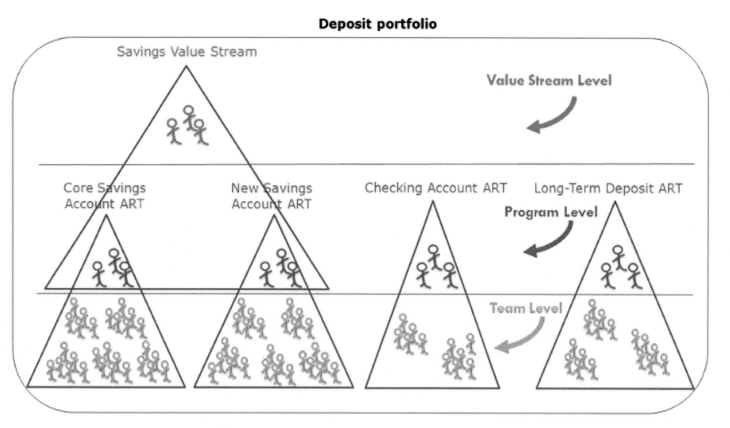

Fig. 26- Deposit Portfolio - Value Stream

We created an imaginary scenario for the bank Deposit portfolio to show that the dependent ARTs are coordinated through the Value Stream Level. But, most of the pure software development teams do not need this Value Stream Level. Typically the Value Stream Level is only needed in complex scenarios where the ARTs need to closely work with other ARTs, such as the development of a large system of systems (solutions) involving software, hardware, and firmware teams. Another example of a complex scenario is the dependency of the ARTs with product-supplier teams who work in a traditional model of software development.

A Value Stream Team is a collection of key stakeholders from ARTs and some additional roles at the Value Stream Level. In summary, SAFe® uses the Agile Team as its primary building block that builds the software. The ART scales multiple Agile Teams and integrates their work into a system. The Value Stream scales multiple ARTs and/or any external teams like suppliers, product vendors, etc. and integrates their work into a solution.

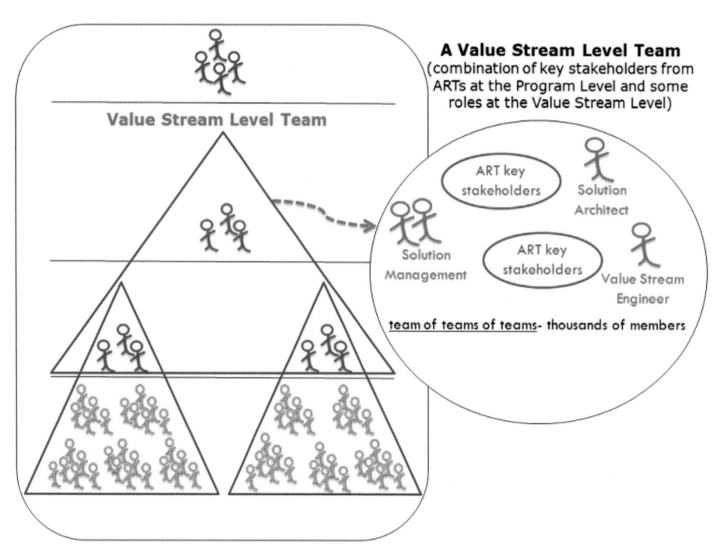

Fig. 27- Value Stream Team structure

Solution Management

This role is similar to the Product Management role. Every Value Stream Team has a Solution Management role which provides the overall solution vision and the top capabilities for the upcoming PI. The Solution Management role can be one person or a group.

Value Stream Engineer (VSE)

This role is similar to the RTE role. VSE is one individual who facilitates the activities of a Value Stream Team.

Solution Architect

This role is similar to the System Architect role. The Solution Architect helps the ARTs to build the architectural and non-functional aspects of the solution and collaborates with the System Architects and Enterprise Architect in evolving the Architectural Runway.

The Schedule

The Value Stream works in the same cadence as the PI. The Value Stream Team provides input to the ARTs before the PI Planning. Similarly the Value Stream Team rolls up the Program PI objectives of its ARTs into the Value Stream PI objectives. In this case, the Value Stream collaborates with the key stakeholders of the ARTs before and after PI Planning through the events called Pre-PI Planning and Post-PI Planning.

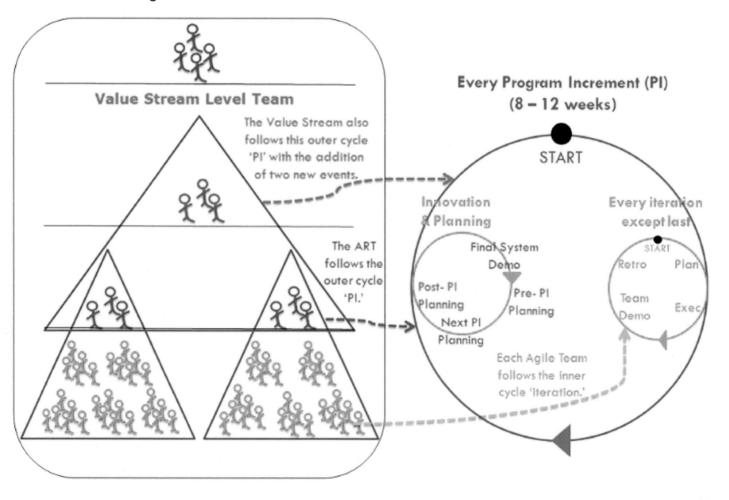

Fig. 28- Value Stream Schedule

The Work

In SAFe®, the upcoming work is organized into backlogs. Each Value Stream Team has a Value Stream Backlog, each ART has a Program Backlog, and each Agile Team has a Team Backlog. The Value Stream Backlog contains '**capabilities**' which are the abstractions of the work. Fig. 29 shows the Value Stream Backlog. Note that the Value Stream Team can also have specialty roles as needed, just like the ARTs.

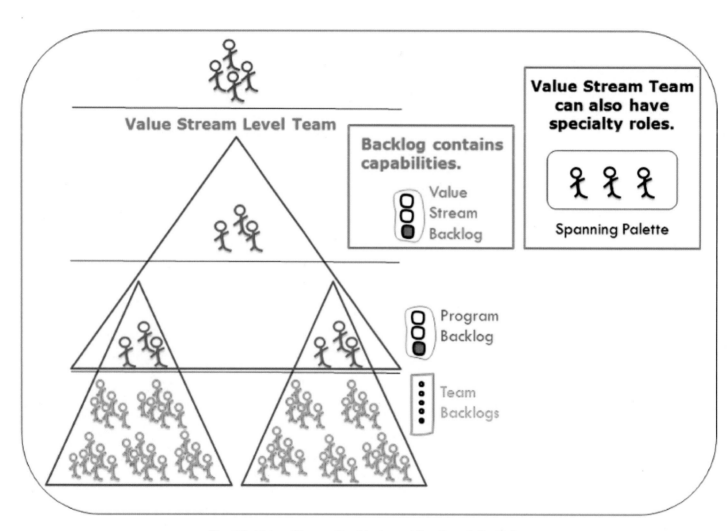

Fig. 29- Value Stream Backlogs and the Specialty Roles

----------Question- 26----------

What unit is used for estimating capabilities?

a) Story Point

b) Use Case Point

c) Function Point

d) Person Hours

-------Answer-------

The Story Point is not only used for estimating the capabilities but also for epics, features, and stories. Stories are estimated in Story Points that are rolled up through features, capabilities, and finally to the epics. Correct answer is 'a.'

----------Question- 26----------

----------Question- 27----------

A Story Point is

a)   An hour of work.

b)   A day of work.

c)   A relative measure of the size of the work.

d)   None of the above.

-------Answer-------

A Story Point is a relative measure to indicate the size of an effort. The size of the effort is independent of the team productivity. Unlike traditional estimates where the original estimations will be re-estimated whenever the team productivity changes, the original estimations in Story Points remain the same even when the productivity of the team changes. Using Story Points, we can track the productivity improvement of the team. When the team productivity increases, the quantum of work completed also increases. Correct answer is 'c.'

----------Question- 27----------

Large developments - Need for Solution Intent and Solution Context

Earlier we discussed that the Value Stream Level is only required for very large developments such as integrated hardware-software systems, firmware, etc. Very large developments build complex solutions, which are systems of systems. For example, if the development goal is to develop a cyber physical solution such as 'auto pilot for an aircraft,' think about the extent of the cross-cutting scope, several teams of specialists, interdisciplinary designs, expensive and complicated test environments, and the resultant need for effective collaboration.

Though Agile Teams do not perform big upfront requirements or designs based on long-term predictions, SAFe® recognizes that very large development contexts require an **optimal**

predictability of solutions requirements, designs, and test strategies. However, it should not become a waterfall approach with big upfront documentation of point (narrow and specific) requirements and designs. It defeats the purpose of being agile. SAFe® chooses a middle path where the Value Stream Team maintains a couple of artifact repositories called Solution Intent and Solution Context. The Solution Intent captures a **set** of business needs rather than a narrow specific business need. It captures a set of alternative designs rather than a narrow specific design.

Having recommended a middle path of upfront documentation of the design alternatives in Solution Intent, SAFe® also suggests ways to increase the usefulness of upfront design artifacts. Instead of text specifications, the team can document or simulate the designs using models. A model can be a model of specification like a UML (Unified Modeling Language), a simulation model like CAD (Computer Aided Design), or a working model like miniatures. Using models to learn about the fitness of the designs is called "*Model-Based Systems Engineering (MBSE).*"

The Solution Context is a repository similar to the Solution Intent. It captures the specifications and constraints about the target environment in which the solution will be deployed (made available in a real environment for end users). For example, in the 'auto pilot' Solution Context, the Value Stream Team must have all the information needed about the deployment environment of the aircraft, such as which external modules and operational infrastructure the auto pilot needs to work with.

OK. Solution Intent is a repository that holds a set of initial alternatives such as business needs, designs, etc. But how will the team finalize the specific design?

The idea behind capturing a set of alternative designs is to keep the options open so that the team can consolidate good design options and eliminate bad design options as they learn. The Value Stream Team will gradually narrow down the set to the right business needs, designs, and tests for the most economical results as the clarity emerges from System Demos during the PI cycles. Starting with a set of alternative designs (variables) and narrowing down to the point designs (fixed) is called "*Set-Based Design.*" This is based on the SAFe® principle, "*Assume variability; preserve options.*"

For example, in the case of 'auto pilot,' it requires a sub system to calculate the weather parameters. To design this sub system, there are multiple technologies to read the input data and multiple algorithms to process the input into weather parameters. It is risky to lock down a specific technology and a specific algorithm as part of the upfront design, as a combination of multiple factors such as vehicle type, intent, usage context, user persona, usage economics, supplier capabilities, etc. make it too complex to predict the design requirements. So, locking down a point design early in such a complex setup is not recommended especially when there are non-negotiable deadlines. The team may not be able to reverse this specific design late in the development when it finds out that the specific design chosen does not meet the real need. So, the team can choose to maintain a set of designs (a combination of different input reading technologies and algorithms) and narrow down to a specific design iteratively as they develop the understanding of the vehicle's behavior in the field.

Value Stream Level vs. Value Stream Team vs. Value Stream

The Value Stream is one of the most difficult concepts to understand in SAFe®. We learned that the Value Stream **Level** is a concept to define empowerment (specific authority), and the Value Stream **Team** is in this level. Apart from the level and the team, SAFe® also uses the core concept of 'Value Stream' extensively to capture a long-lived process along with systems and people around this process through which an enterprise delivers value in response to a customer request. Some examples of the Value Streams include the core business activities of the enterprise such as 'providing marketing offers,' 'selling products,' 'servicing the customers,' etc. This distinction is important to know since 'Value Streams' are excellent abstractions of how enterprises work and can serve as a tool for analysis and improvement of the enterprise. You are encouraged to learn more about the 'Value Streams' separately after understanding the basics of SAFe®.

----------Question- 28----------

Choose the incorrect statement about the Value Streams.

   a)   In SAFe®, Value Streams and ARTs are funded.

   b)   Value Streams refer to the business requirements at the Value Stream Level.

   c)   Value Streams are abstractions of how value is built in enterprises. The value flow depicted in a Value Stream is amenable for end-to-end analysis and identification of delays.

   d)   None of the above.

-------Answer-------

In SAFe®, Value Streams and ARTs are funded. Value Streams are good abstractions for the end-to-end analysis of how the value flows and identification of any delays to the flow. The 'capabilities' (not the Value Streams) are the abstractions that capture the business requirements at the Value Stream Level. Correct answer is 'b.'

----------Question- 28----------

##

The Portfolio

The Agile Team builds the software. The ART, which is a long-lived team of Agile Teams, integrates and delivers the work of multiple Agile Teams into a system. The Value Stream scales the ARTs and integrates the work of multiple ARTs into a solution. Both the Value Stream Team and the ARTs work in the same fixed time schedule called the PI, which is a learning cycle that repeats. The Value Stream, ART, and Agile Teams organize their work in a Value Stream Backlog, Program Backlog, and Team Backlog. The Value Stream Team provides the input to the PI Planning by selecting capabilities from the Value Stream Backlog. The ART plans the scope of the PI by selecting features from the Program Backlog. The Agile Team plans the scope of the iterations by selecting stories from the Team Backlog.

In some portfolios of the enterprise there may be one or more Value Stream Teams (portfolios implementing SAFe® 4 Level). In other portfolios, there may be just one or more ARTs without Value Stream Levels (portfolios implementing SAFe® 3 Level). In either case, who provides the overall strategy and the direction of the portfolio? Who is responsible for keeping the teams funded and ensuring that the teams are working on the right functional and technical initiatives? Who is responsible for updating the external stakeholders about the plan and status of the portfolio? A large team of teams with hundreds and thousands of team members will go out of alignment with the organization's mission if someone does not take a focused responsibility on the above aspects. The Portfolio Team is that someone.

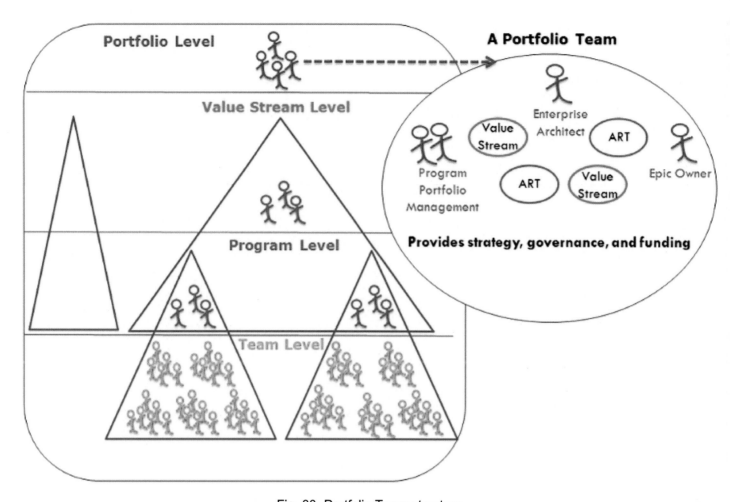

Fig. 30- Portfolio Team structure

Program Portfolio Management (PPM)

This is a role mostly played by a group of people with the highest strategic and financial authority in the portfolio. It may consist of the following.

•   Executives who formulate strategic themes and allocate funds.

•   The Program Management Office (PMO) that supports the program execution by standardizing effective practices.

•   Others as needed for the stakeholder governance and reporting.

Epic Owner

The Epic Owner tracks the epics from analysis all the way through implementation and closure. It can be taken up by anyone from any level. Once the epic is completed, they can once again choose to be an Epic Owner for another epic or opt not to.

Enterprise Architect

The Enterprise Architect is responsible for consistent standards of the technical stack, the infrastructure across the portfolio, and provides guidance on the common design and component patterns.

The Schedule

The portfolio does not follow the PI or iteration. The Portfolio Team adjusts the budget once or twice a year.

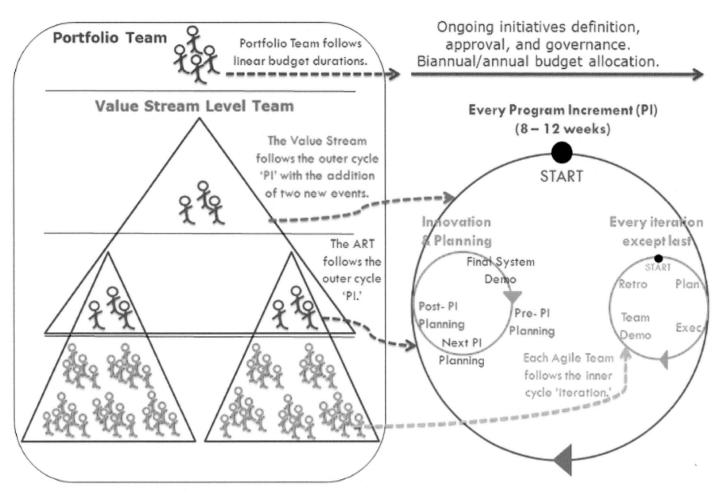

Fig. 31- Portfolio Schedule

The Work

In SAFe® the upcoming work is organized as backlogs. Just like the teams at other levels, the Portfolio Team has a Portfolio Backlog that carries a list of epics. An epic is an abstraction of a large cross-cutting initiative whose work may require a 6 to 9 month period. The Portfolio Team is guided by a set of strategic themes to define the epics. Strategic themes are derived from the organization's strategies, and they provide the direction for the future of the portfolio.

----------Question- 29----------

Epic, which represents a large initiative, is only defined in the Portfolio Backlog.

a) True

b) False

-------Answer-------

Local epics may be identified at the Value Stream and Program Levels also. They are contained in the Value Stream Backlog and the Program Backlog respectively. The Program Portfolio Management, however, is still the approval authority of these local epics. Correct answer is 'b.'

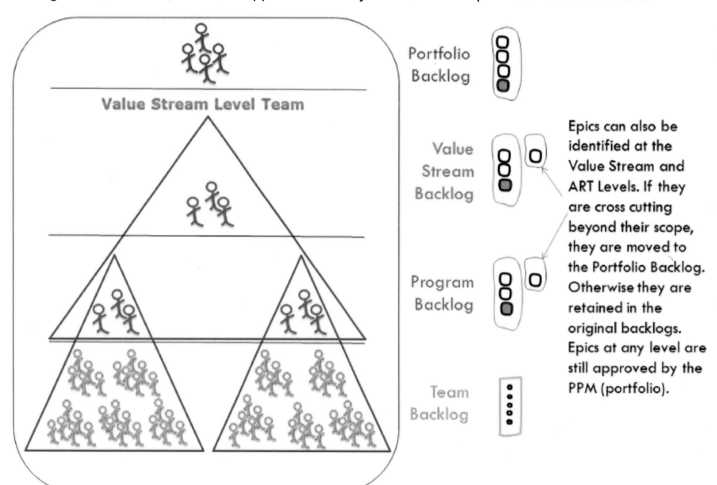

Fig. 32- Portfolio Backlogs and Epics

----------Question- 29----------

The terms for work types are interesting, but some real-world examples would help...

Practical Peter

For an enterprise which is **product centric** today, one of the strategic themes can be '*Revamp the internal and external structures and solutions around **customer centricity**.*' This strategic theme expresses the direction for the future and a desired future differentiation. Strategic themes provide the context for decision-making at different levels within the portfolio.

For a portfolio with 'customer centricity' as a strategic theme, *'Establish a data warehouse infrastructure for customer insights*' can be an example epic. Obviously this epic like every epic is a cross-cutting large initiative that requires thorough analysis before approval and funding. To aid with decision-making, Epic Owners facilitate the creation of success criteria and a lightweight business case for each epic. The PPM reviews the success criteria and the lightweight business case before the epic approval.

Assuming that the enterprise is building intelligent machines with embedded software, '*Build a live usage data broadcast module*' can be an example of a capability. Note that this capability like every capability appears to be a combination of software and devices.

'*A dashboard that shows a 360 degree view of a customer*' can be an example of a feature. Note that most features sound like typical product features in marketing brochures.

'*As a marketing analyst, I would like to search for a specific customer by customer id, so that I can view their contact information*' can be an example of a story. Note how much granular detail a story gets. Such granularity facilitates easy understanding, estimation, and potential ownership by a small team.

How the value flows together from the enterprise through the portfolio to the customers

Lean-Agile Budgeting:

The enterprise allocates a lump sum budget for each of the portfolios. Each portfolio is then responsible for realizing the solutions to meet a set of enterprise business strategies. Once the enterprise allocates the lump sum budget, the Portfolio Team is empowered to make subsequent funding allocations and decisions within the portfolio.

Unlike traditional budgeting where each project will be funded, the portfolio will fund the Value Streams or ARTs in that portfolio. The funding is done for six months and can be adjusted in the next six months.

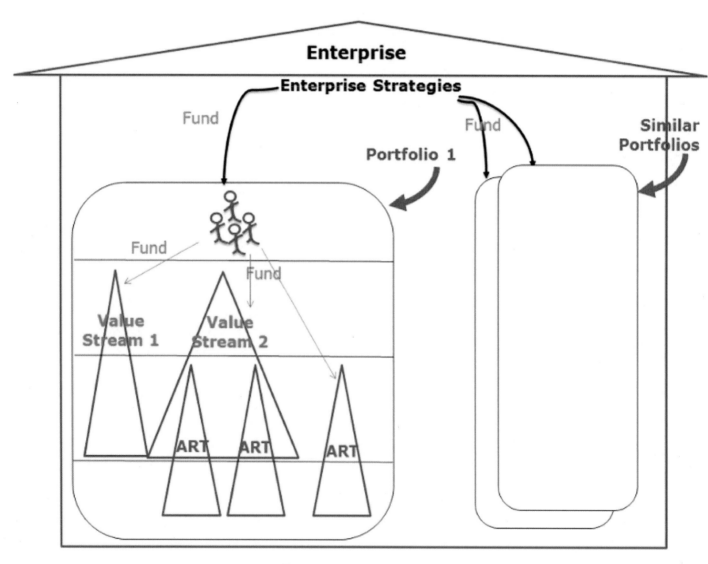

Fig. 33- Portfolio Budgeting

The portfolio allocates budget to the Value Stream, and the Value Stream spends it. I don't understand how this is different from traditional budgeting.

There are two key differences between Lean-Agile Budgeting and traditional budgeting. In Lean-Agile Budgeting, the Value Streams or ARTs, both being team of teams, are funded and the work is brought to the teams, whereas in traditional budgeting the projects (work) are funded, and the teams are brought to the work. So Lean-Agile Budgeting reduces the complexities around resource estimation, staffing, and ongoing demand management. The second difference is Lean-Agile Budgeting allows spending empowerment for the teams that are closer to the work. Just like a Portfolio Team is empowered to make funding decisions related to the Value Streams and ARTs, the Value Stream leadership and ART leadership can decide which capabilities and features will be funded. For example, in Fig. 34 a Value Stream gets a lump sum allocation from the portfolio for a couple of PIs. This Value Stream has two ARTs. It is up to the Value Stream leadership to decide which features of which ART need to be prioritized for funding decisions. If one of the ARTs needs more money to complete a high-priority feature, it can be obtained by stopping some low-priority features in other ARTs. This provides the local agility to respond to emerging opportunities. In traditional budgeting if a project needs more money, it must undergo several change management procedures in the higher levels of the hierarchy.

However, Lean-Agile Budgeting does not giving full freedom to local teams on spending. SAFe® enables the Portfolio Team to retain the spending control on large initiatives like epics.

Every epic must be approved by the Program Portfolio Management (PPM). Once approved, the epic will be locally funded by the respective Value Stream. Usually the epics originate at the Portfolio Level. Epics, however, can also be found at the Value Stream Level and the Program Level. These epics need to be analyzed, reviewed, and approved by the PPM. Newly found portfolio epics will be funded from a budgetary reserve, while local epics (Value Stream and Program epics) will be funded from the Value Stream budgets.

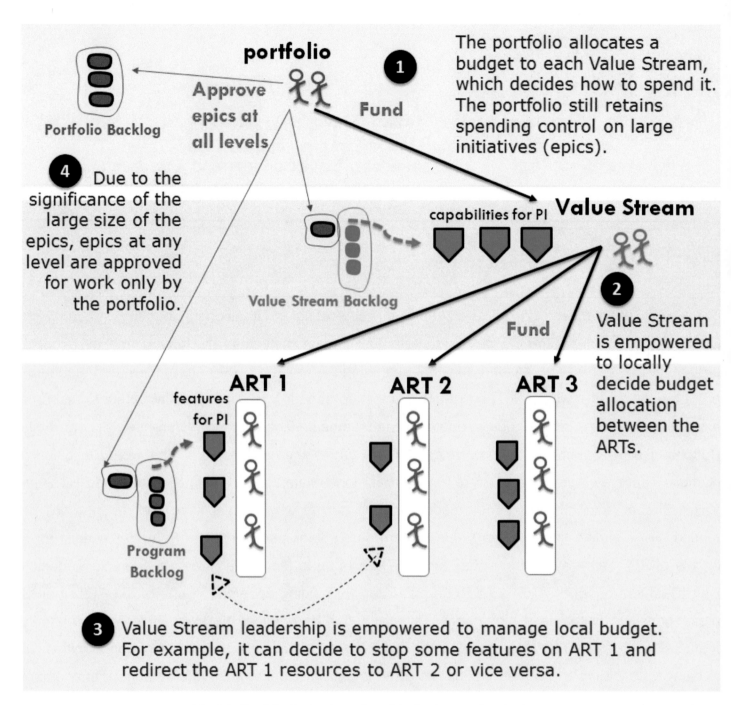

Fig. 34- Portfolio Budgeting – Local Authority to adjust budgets

From the accounting perspective, the budget expenditure can be from the Operational Expense Budget (Opex) or the Capital Expense Budget (Capex). Until the epic is approved and moved into the Portfolio Backlog, the expense is considered an Opex. The cost associated with the development of this epic is considered a Capex. The funding allocated to the Value Stream includes both Opex and Capex.

----------Question- 30----------

In Lean-Agile Budgeting, budgets are allocated to the

a)   Backlogs.

b) PI.

c) Value Streams.

d) Projects.

-------Answer-------

In traditional budgeting, projects are funded. In SAFe®, the enterprise allocates a lump sum budget to each portfolio. Within each portfolio, this budget is allocated between the Value Streams and ARTs. Correct answer is 'c.'

----------Question- 30----------

Decentralized Decision-Making:

Within the portfolio, the work and the value flow through Kanban. Fig. 35 shows how the work flows through Kanban from left to right in each level. For example, in the Portfolio Level business initiatives are captured in the first step of the Kanban workflow called the 'Funnel.' Then they pass through the 'Review' and the 'Analysis' steps. Once approved for implementation, they move to the Portfolio Backlog as epics. At the boundary of the next PI, the teams in the next level pull the work into their Kanban. For example, at the PI boundary an ART pulls the top decomposed capabilities (features) from the Value Stream Backlog into the Program Kanban. Just before the PI Planning, a sufficient number of features are approved into the Program Backlog so that they can be addressed in PI Planning. In PI Planning, the ART collaborates, plans, and commits the scope of what it will develop in the upcoming PI. Through this event, the features from the Program Backlog will move to the Team Backlog as stories. Note how the teams are authorized to own and manage decisions on their content (backlog) at each level. This is based on the SAFe® principle, "*Decentralize decision-making.*"

A combination of various SAFe® aspects such as Lean-Agile Budgeting, specific decision authority provided for the teams at each level, and the practice of prioritization using Weighted Shortest Job First (WSJF) is called the "*Economic Framework.*" The "*Economic Framework*" brings in objectivity and clarity for the teams at the different levels to make quick and economically sensible decisions. In effect, this encourages decentralized decision-making. The SAFe® "Economic Framework" is only a framework (not a prescription). Enterprises can customize or add more local guidelines in order to provide a contextually relevant framework for the teams to analyze and respond to the emerging situations from an economical angle.

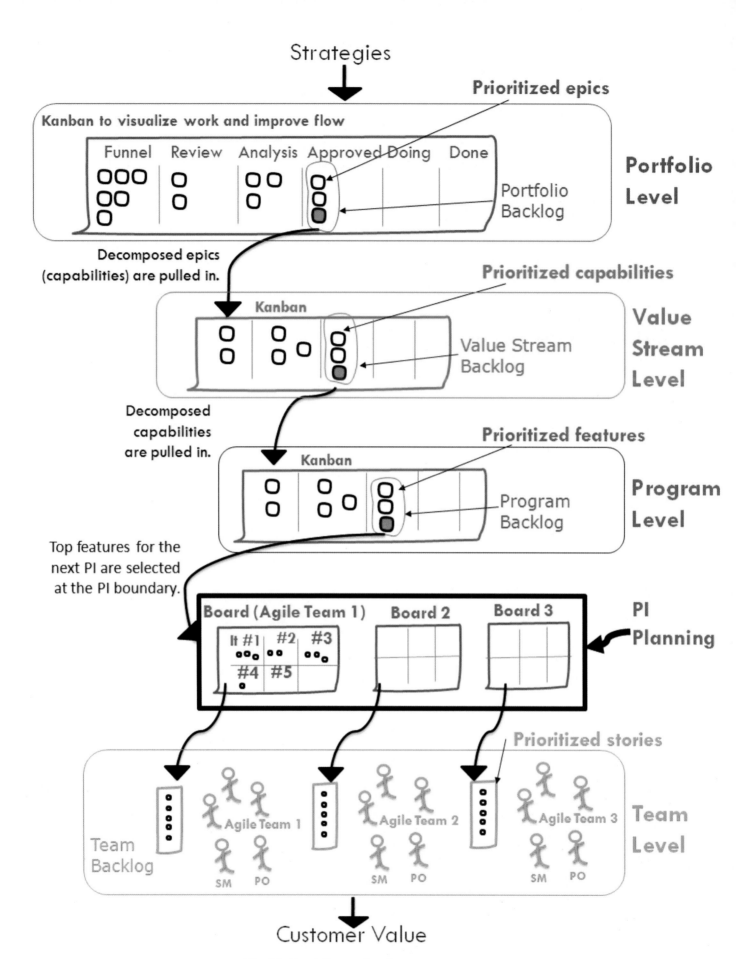

Fig. 35- Portfolio – value flows through Kanban

Notice how the Kanban aspects help

- To increase the visibility of work and its flow.

- To set the maximum limit of how many items can be developed (limiting Work-In-Process) in each Kanban step. Setting the limit nudges the teams to complete the 'in-process' items before taking on more. This ensures an increased completion rate and overall flow. This is based on the first part of the SAFe® principle, "*Visualize and limit WIP, reduce batch sizes, and manage queue lengths.*"

----------Question- 31----------

Select two choices. Limiting the Work-In-Process (WIP) expedites the delivery by promoting

a) Throughput.

b) Collaboration.

c) Code Quality.

d) Automation.

-------Answer-------

WIP makes the team complete the 'in-process' items completely before they can take up the next. So it increases the throughput and team collaboration which leads to quicker deliveries. Correct answers are 'a' and 'b.'

----------Question- 31----------

----------Question- 32----------

The 'Funnel' step of the Portfolio Kanban does not have WIP limits.

a) True

b) False

-------Answer-------

Setting a WIP limit, i.e. defining the maximum number of items that can be developed in parallel in a Kanban step, prevents the team from starting several items. Working several items together reduces the undivided time an item gets and hence increases the duration of its completion. Limiting the WIP is a practice in Kanban that enables the team to focus on finishing the work before it takes up new work. In turn, finishing the work faster increases the flow of the work items. While other steps such as 'Review' and 'Analysis' have WIP limits, the 'Funnel' does not have a WIP limit. The 'Funnel' is intentionally kept without a limit because it is the starting point of the portfolio. Any number of potential epics (business needs and ideas) can be added for further consideration. Correct answer is 'a.'

----------Question- 32----------

"Working several items together reduces the undivided time an item gets and hence increases the duration of its completion." Does this contradict the previous question about waterfalling the iteration?

Dividing a story into tasks such as requirements, analysis, design, test, etc. and completing them one by one in sequence is called waterfalling the iteration. Completing one of the above tasks gives a false sense of completion because the story is not complete until all the tasks are finished. For an Agile Team, it is essential to work on them in parallel to complete the story early in order to demonstrate the value. WIP on the other hand limits starting so many items in parallel in order to increase the focus and flow. An Agile Team must strike a balance by choosing a limit that allows enough tasks for all the team members yet ensures sufficient focus for the tasks.

Appropriate Sizing:

To enable the continuous flow within the portfolio, the backlog items need to be decomposed to appropriate sizes. Appropriate sizing allows the teams at a certain level to complete an item within the schedule followed at that level. For example, a feature that requires a duration of more than the length of a PI is not appropriately sized. It must be decomposed further such that it fits in the PI timeframe. Fig. 36 shows both the backlog at each level and the maximum size allowed for the items within that backlog.

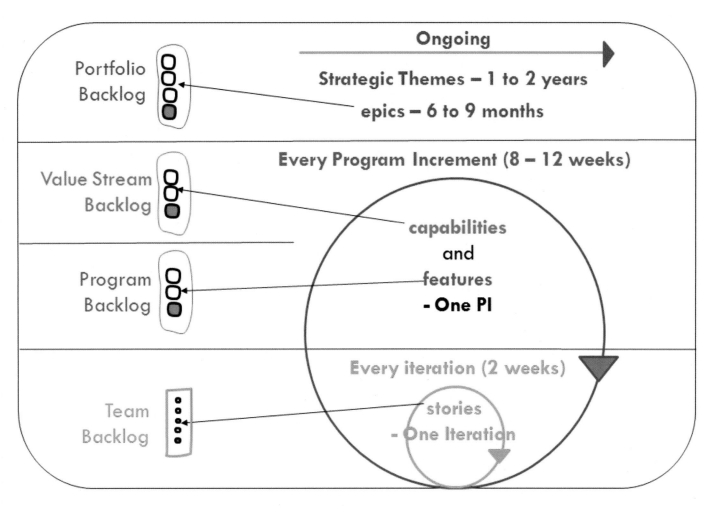

Fig. 36- Size of the backlog items

##

SAFe® Elements in a Nutshell

Here is a recap of the work items in SAFe®.

Work abstraction	What is it?	Where does it come from?	How is it different?
Strategic Theme	An objective that clearly articulates a strategic differentiation that the enterprise needs to create in the future.	Derived from the overall organizational strategies.	Unlike the epic/capability/feature/story, it does not indicate the work to be performed but defines a portfolio focused interest area for direction.
Epic	A large initiative that warrants analysis and funding approval.	Put together by portfolio stakeholders guided by strategic themes. Can also be identified at the Value Stream Level or Program Level.	While a strategic theme is an expression of a high-level direction setter, an epic is treated like a traditional project of less than a year with estimates and benefits.
Capability	An abstraction more granular than an epic, but not as detailed as features.	Can be decomposed from a parent epic or locally identified (hence no parent epic).	While an epic is a large initiative, cross-cutting different Value Streams, a capability is a business solution within a specific Value Stream developed within one Program Increment.
Feature	A 'feature' in the traditional sense used in product/service brochures.	Can be decomposed from a parent epic or capability or locally identified (hence no parent).	While a capability falls within a specific Value Stream, it can span ARTs. A feature is appropriately sized such that it can be developed by one ART in one PI.
Story	A carrier of a user value expressed in a simple statement like 'As a <User Role>, I would like <specific outcome> so that <expected benefit>.'	Can be decomposed from a parent feature or locally identified (hence no parent).	While a feature can be large enough to be developed in a Program Increment, a story is appropriately sized such that it can be developed by one Agile Team in one iteration.

----------Question- 33----------

Why can't backlogs be compared with queues?

a) Queues always follow first in first out, but backlogs are continuously re-prioritized.

b) Backlogs always follow first in first out, but queues are continuously re-prioritized.

c) Backlogs are requirement specifications. Queues are work items.

d) None of the above.

-------Answer-------

Backlogs are continuously reprioritized whereas queues follow the first in first out (FIFO) approach.
Such continuous reprioritization helps the business to inject high-priority items into the backlog and

have them selected for the next planning. Also, the backlogs are pruned appropriately removing low-value items so that the backlogs do not become excessively lengthy which increases the wait time for a new work item to be taken up. This is based on the last part of the SAFe® principle, "*Visualize and limit WIP, reduce batch sizes, and manage queue lengths*." Correct answer is 'a.'

----------Question- 33----------

----------Question- 34----------

SAFe® backlogs are ordered based on

a)   Value.

b)   Cost.

c)   Discretion of the Product Owner.

d)   Weighted Shortest Job First (WSJF).

   -------Answer-------

The parameter used to order the items within a backlog is called Weighted Shortest Job First (WSJF). WSJF is mandatory for all the backlogs except the Team Backlog. For the Team Backlog it is only recommended. WSJF is an index for each item in the backlog. Choosing to work on a work item with a lower WSJF than another item of the same size but with a higher WSJF means - **we are choosing to trade a higher value for a lower value**. In other words, we are incurring more cost of delay.

WSJF is a formula; WSJF = Cost of Delay / Job Size.

The WSJF index indicates that a work item is collectively more valuable in terms of not just the individual business value but along with timeliness (how quickly it needs to be worked to get more value) and the opportunity it offers to reduce risk or exploit a positive change. Using WSJF to prioritize the backlog items is based on the SAFe® principle, "*Take an economic view*." Correct answer is 'd.'

----------Question- 34----------

----------Question- 35----------

Who can approve an epic for implementation?

a)   Agile Release Train

b)   Agile Team

c) Program Portfolio Management (PPM)

----------Question- 35----------

That's a lot of mathematics. An example of calculating a WSJF would really help!

Practical Peter

In simple terms it is enough to understand that to maximize the value creation, an item with a higher WSJF needs to be worked before another item with a lower WSJF. WSJF is calculated from a set of parameters.

WSJF = Cost of Delay / Job Size.

Cost of Delay = Business Value + Timeliness + Opportunity of exploiting or reducing a risk.

Job Size refers to the time needed to develop an item.

Business Value refers to the direct business benefits expected from the item, such as revenue, cost savings, etc.

Timeliness refers to how quickly an item needs to be brought to market.

Opportunity of exploiting or reducing a risk is also called Risk Reduction/Opportunity Enablement (RR/OE).

Each of these parameters - Job Size, Business Value, Timeliness, and RR/OE - can be a relative number. Relevant numbers can be from the set of Fibonacci numbers: 1, 2, 3, 5, 8, 13, 21, 34, etc.

Let's take three work items and calculate their WSJF.

Item Description	Business Value	Timeliness (Time Criticality)	RR/ OE	Cost of Delay (CoD) - add all three	Job Size	WSJF = CoD/Job Size
A production defect preventing 5 users per day from completing a critical transaction.	8	13	13	34	5	6.8
A production defect showing an irrelevant message to 10 users per day.	2	5	1	8	2	4
A new business feature that will persuade 5 users per day to switch from the competition.	13	8	5	26	13	2

Even without the calculation, it is evident that the first item, a critical production defect, must be addressed first. WSJF confirms that finding. The second item, a low-value production defect, on the other hand appears to be less important than the third item, a new business feature which would bring in new users. But, the smaller job size and hence the higher WSJF makes it clear that the second item will produce a quicker value.

SAFe® Principles

1. Take an economic view

Maximize the economic value by making trade offs between risk, cost of delay, and operation and development cost.

Applied: Economic Framework (Combination of SAFe® aspects such as Lean-Agile Budgeting, delegation of specific responsibilities to the teams, WSJF, etc. that help the teams to apply an economic view)

2. Apply systems thinking

Treating the organization that builds the solution, the solution itself, and the Value Streams, through which the organization delivers the solutions to users, as a system of systems.

Applied: Value Streams, Portfolio

3. Assume variability; preserve options

Accepting that we cannot predict the solution upfront, starting with a set of alternative solutions and narrowing them down as we learn.

Applied: Set Based Design, Model-Based Systems Engineering (MBSE)

4. Build incrementally with fast, integrated learning cycles

Time-boxed iterations to reduce risk, building incremental value by rapid feedback, and course corrections.

Applied: Outer cycle (PI), Inner cycle (iteration)

5. Base milestones on objective evaluation of working systems

Working systems are the only mark of progress. They are the objective evidence of return on investment.

Applied: Demonstrations at the cycle boundaries

6. Visualize and limit WIP, reduce batch sizes, and manage queue lengths

Increasing the flow by limiting the work within the capacity, reducing the size of work batches, and reducing the length of the committed work queue.

Applied: Backlog grooming and management through Kanban

7. Apply cadence, synchronize with cross-domain planning

Having predictable repetition of events to sync up by cadence (calibrating the events to start, frequently meet, end at the same time) and synchronization (people from different domains coming together to reduce differences).

Applied: SAFe® cycles bringing all the people together in defined and repeating events

8. Unlock the intrinsic motivation of knowledge workers

Motivating by providing opportunities to solve problems and liberating bottom-up intelligence.

Applied: Self-organized and cross-functional teams of teams

9. Decentralize decision-making

Real-time and local context based decision-making.

Applied: Levels with clear responsibilities and authority, Economic Framework

How the roles compare between different levels

We now understand all of the SAFe® Level roles. Here is the recap.

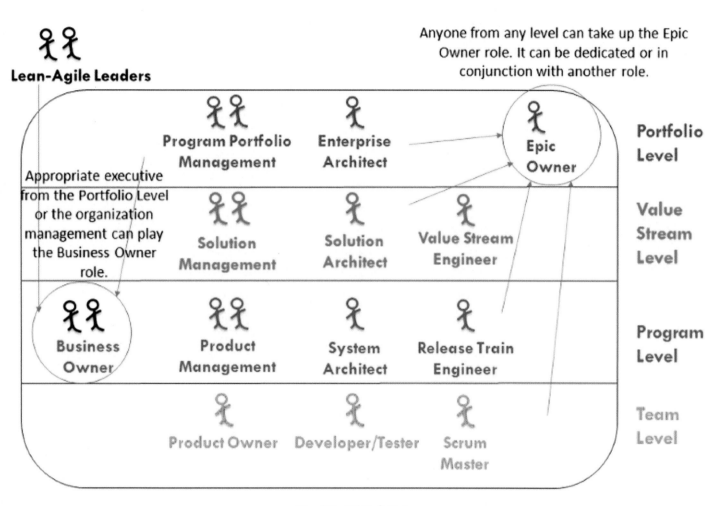

Fig. 37- SAFe® Roles

Lean-Agile Leader and the SAFe® House of Lean

Note that there is also a role called **Lean-Agile Leader** in Fig. 37. Lean-Agile Leaders refer to the organization management at different levels. Management in SAFe® does not follow the traditional command style from the top. Instead management consists of Lean-Agile Leaders who follow Lean and Agile principles, communicate the vision to the teams, facilitate the open collaboration, remove the organization-level impediments, and create an environment for everyone to follow Lean-Agile principles and practices. In short, Lean-Agile Leaders do not work as commanders or coordinators, but model their behavior as developers of people exhibiting Lean-Agile thinking.

Lean-Agile thinking is a combination of The Agile Manifesto values and principles and the "*SAFe® House of Lean*." We previously discussed The Agile Manifesto. The "*SAFe® House of Lean*" has a structure made of a foundation block, four pillars, and a roof.

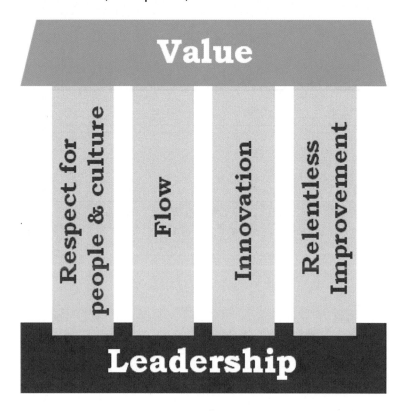

Fig. 38- The SAFe® House of Lean

The "*SAFe® House of Lean*" clearly specifies how a Lean-Agile Leader should think and exhibit the required behavior to lead the transformation. The foundation is Lean-Agile Leadership, indicating that leaders are directly in charge of driving change. They are responsible for the adoption of the Lean-Agile culture. This is evident in the fact that SAFe® installs leaders (management) in leading roles at every level. The roof signifies the goal that Lean-Agile Leaders should strive for value. The leader should be ready to make organizational level changes to deliver the maximum value in the sustainably shortest lead time with the best quality and value to people and society. Value as the goal is evident in most of the SAFe® principles and the SAFe® value "*Alignment*."

SAFe® Pillars

1. Respect for people and culture

While the leaders coach the people, they need to groom the culture, where people get the empowerment to decide how to perform their work and troubleshoot issues.

Source: Reflects in specific principles like "*Unlock the intrinsic motivation of knowledge workers*," "*Decentralize decision-making*," and the SAFe® value "*Transparency*"

2. Flow

Leaders should restructure the existing product development process and practices to facilitate continuous flow of value unlike projects that have irregular start-stop movements.

Source: Reflects in most of the principles and the values *"Built-in Quality"* and *"Program Execution"*

3. Innovation

Leaders should be on the ground, learn through cycles, and be ready to make course corrections. Leaders should provide time and space for people to innovate.

Source: Reflects in SAFe® building blocks where leaders closely collaborate with teams and in the dedicated IP iteration for experimental learning

4. Relentless improvement

Leaders should facilitate stepping back often, reflecting, learning, and improving.

Source: Reflects in some of the SAFe® Principles

----------Question- 36----------

A critical contributor to the *"Relentless Improvement"* pillar is

a) Retrospective.

b) Daily Stand-ups.

c) PI Planning.

-------Answer-------

"Relentless Improvement" is one of the pillars of the *"SAFe® House of Lean."* It involves retrospectives at milestones and continuous improvement techniques. Correct answer is 'a.'

----------Question- 36----------

All the roles

The number of roles in SAFe® is unusually high for an Agile framework. It is a bit overwhelming initially to understand all of the roles. To aid in a firm understanding, here is a comparison of the roles together with a crisp description of each.

	Individual or Group?	With whom do they mostly collaborate to get direction?	What is their top responsibility?
PPM	Group	Enterprise	Portfolio Strategy, Execution, and Governance.
Enterprise Architect	Individual	Enterprise Strategy	Establishing common infrastructure and reusable patterns.
Epic Owner	Individual	PMO (that works as part of PPM)	Tracking epic to completion.
Product Management	Group	PPM	Maintaining Roadmap and providing near-term vision.
RTE	Individual	PMO	Facilitating ART's progress by removing impediments.
System Architect	Individual	Enterprise Architect	Establishing common architecture at the system and sub-system level.
Business Owner	Group	Enterprise	Providing long-term vision.
Agile Team	Group	Product Owner	Create integrated increments at every iteration.
Product Owner	Individual	Product Management	Maintaining and providing near-term product plan.
Scrum Master	Individual	RTE	Facilitating Agile Team's progress by removing impediments.

Since most of the roles at the Value Stream Level are very similar to the roles at the Program Level, the comparison has not included the Value Stream roles.

In addition to these primary roles, SAFe® also offers a list of specialty roles that can be added to the Value Stream or Program Levels as required. In SAFe®'s "*Big Picture*," these roles are shown separately in a section called "*Spanning Palette*." Fig. 39 shows these additional specialty roles.

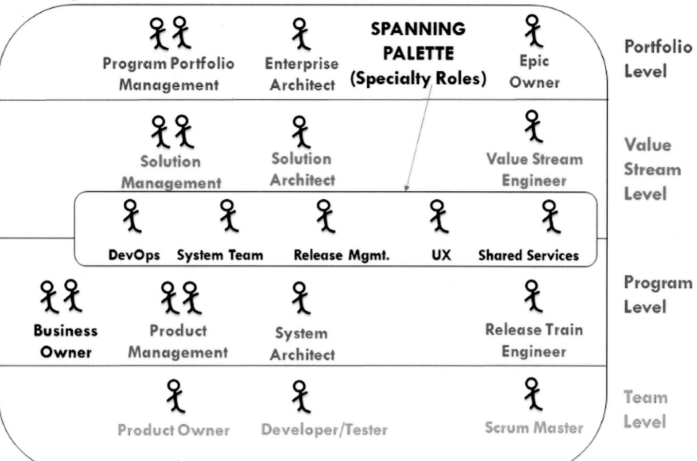

Fig. 39- SAFe® – All the Roles

##

Transformation to SAFe® - FAQ

SAFe® touches all aspects of an organization. Which aspects are mandatory for a successful implementation?

In addition to Agile, SAFe® uses many concepts from Lean and Systems Thinking. Instead of choosing to apply all the concepts, a SAFe® implementation can be customized. In fact, SAFe® leaves the transformation and implementation approach to the organization in order to customize it to best suit their needs. Though SAFe® can be customized, Scaled Agile does not explicitly identify which aspects are immutable and which can be modified. Yet, we can think about certain foundational elements that are critical to SAFe® effectiveness and hence cannot be compromised. Three sources that hold the essence of SAFe® are (1) SAFe® House of Lean (2) SAFe® Core Values (3) SAFe® Principles. It is essential that any customized SAFe® implementation respects them. Here are some examples of customizations and whether they are good choices or not.

Customization	Inference
An ART has five teams which do PI Planning together, but they choose not to integrate every iteration nor hold a System Demo.	This violates the SAFe® principle, "Build incrementally with fast, integrated learning cycles." By not integrating every iteration, the teams lose the learning opportunity and accumulate risk. This is a bad customization.
An ART has chosen to ignore the formulation of Team and Program PI Objectives.	PI Objectives are a great means to verify a team's understanding of the business objectives. It ensures the alignment between the business leadership and the ART. This violates the SAFe® core value "Alignment." This is a bad customization.
An ART has chosen to embed a User Experience (UX) expert within each Agile Team rather than having a common UX at the Program Level.	There is no evidence of violation of the essence of SAFe®. If the needs make sense to embed UX into the Agile teams, it is acceptable.

Are there other patterns for implementing SAFe® other than "Implementing SAFe® 1-2-3"?

Fig. 40 shows three possible patterns including the "Implementing SAFe® 1-2-3" steps (Pattern 1). Scaled Agile recommends Pattern 1 although they do not position it as the only transformation approach. Patterns 2 and 3 are more aggressive alternatives added by the author. In the author's experience an organization may start with a more aggressive approach than Pattern 1 for strategic reasons. Also, an organization that started its first implementation with an ART in a portfolio (Pattern 1) may choose to go for a full portfolio implementation for the next portfolio. These three approaches differ only in their starting point and their associated risks. Patterns 2 and 3 are more aggressive approaches and hence riskier compared to Pattern 1 in the transformation to SAFe®. All three approaches allow the organization to Inspect and Adapt gradually.

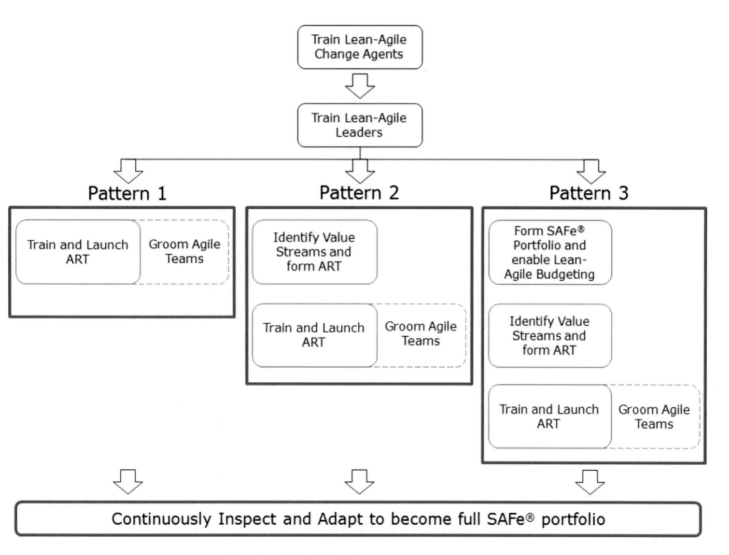

Fig. 40- SAFe® Implementation Patterns

An organization may start with a more aggressive approach than Pattern 1, but only after carefully considering the pros and cons.

Pattern 2 helps to address the ART's longevity problem present in Pattern 1. Pattern 2 starts with the analysis of the existing organization from the Value Stream perspective. It identifies the potential

Value Streams around which the ARTs can be formed. Pattern 2 provides an opportunity to organize long-lived teams around these Value Streams to support perennial initiatives rather than repeatedly forming and dissolving short-lived teams.

Pattern 3 is about a full implementation of a SAFe® portfolio. This requires active support and involvement from the organization's management as well as those in business and technology.

The pros and cons of each implementation follow.

SAFe® Transformation Pattern 1

Pros:

- It is not an Enterprise Level change so it is relatively easy to start with an ART for one program.

- Initial ARTs are usually formed around existing team patterns. Newly found ways of larger and open collaboration like combined PI Planning and dependency management will bring quick benefits.

Cons:

- This is largely an IT transformation. Business functions like program management will continue to work in the old ways.

- Longevity of the ART is questionable since the ART may have been formed around existing teams instead of around Value Streams.

SAFe® Transformation Pattern 2

Pros:

- Forming ARTs around the Value Stream increases the chance of a long-term domain knowledge of the team. It allows better team alignment to the value produced by the organization.

- Value Streams are great abstractions that are amenable for analysis to find ways of improving speed, efficiency, and quality of the value delivered.

Cons:

- The Value Stream is one of most complex concepts in SAFe®. Identification and defragmentation of the Value Streams requires Value Stream experts.

- Many organizations do not have defined Value Streams with clear boundaries. Any attempt to revamp the existing ecosystem around the Value Streams may be a structural change.

SAFe® Transformation Pattern 3

Pros:

- Implementing full SAFe® with the Portfolio Level, Value Stream Level (optional), Program Level, and Team Level helps to expedite the flow of value from the strategic layer to the user layer. It brings better alignment between those responsible for the organizational strategy and performance and those who actually execute on the ground to realize these strategies.

•	There are many opportunities for visualizing the issues in the path of the end-to-end flow of value and collaborating to make dramatic improvements because of the close proximity and active participation of the stakeholders and decision makers.

Cons:

•	This is a massive transformation to many functions of the organization. Not only product development but also sales, marketing, finance, and portfolio management must adjust their current way of working. Lack of executive support and broad change management will be detrimental.

•	There are many aspects around team structure, roles, activities, and artifacts that need to change altogether, and this change may turn out to be more complex than originally understood.

##

Circling Back

We started the book with a set of questions that arose when small Agile Teams needed to scale. Here is a recap of the questions for you to review.

- What are the roles and responsibilities of the organization's management?

- How to align the Agile Teams to the corporate strategies?

- How to cascade these strategies to the hundreds of Agile Teams?

- How can different business owners, who have different needs that impact the same set of Agile Teams, collaborate?

- How to integrate the work performed by different Agile Teams?

- How to integrate support teams like Technology Architecture, User Experience, Project Management Office, etc.?

- How to align the upstream business functions, such as portfolio management and program management, with the Agile Teams?

SAFe® tries to answer these questions by providing a framework of team of teams, levels, work backlogs, roles, and activities along with the values and principles that bind them together. You have acquired a fundamental knowledge of SAFe® now. The skeleton version of the SAFe® framework is summarized in Fig. 41.

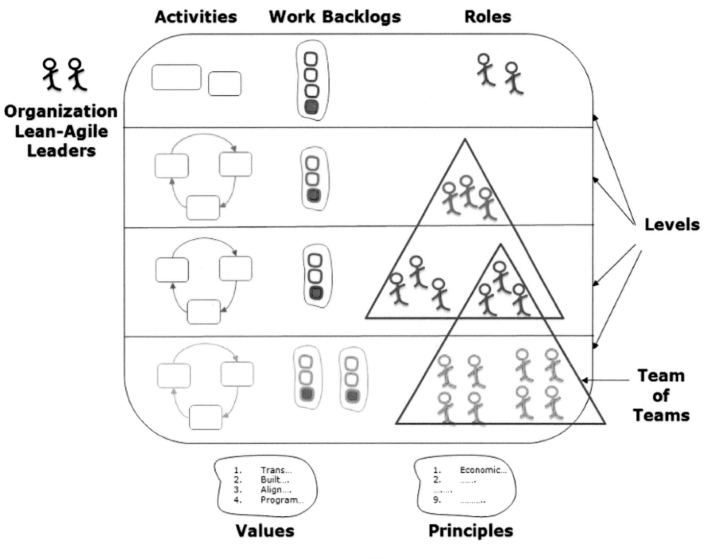

Fig. 41- The SAFe® framework

This knowledge will help you to explore the "*Big Picture*" shown in Fig. 42 which is available in an interactive format at http://www.scaledagileframework.com. The knowledge from this book will be also useful before and after SAFe® training sessions.

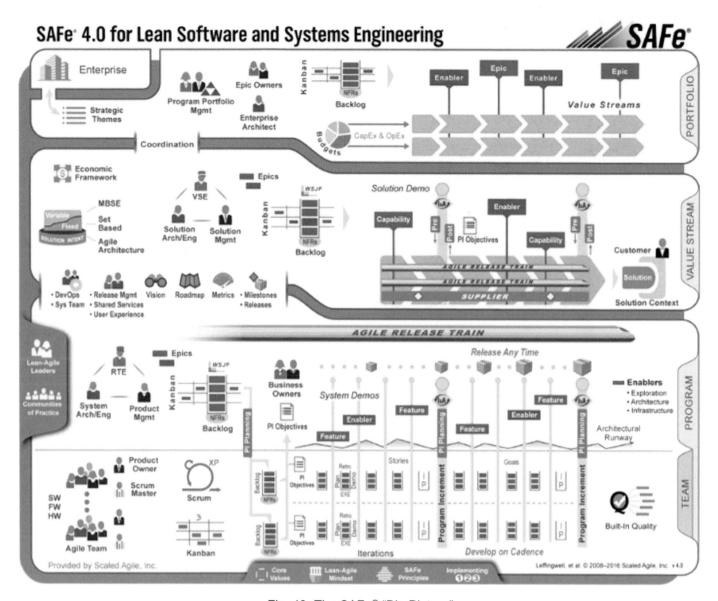

Fig. 42- The SAFe® "Big Picture"

##

Journey to Excellence is a Path. Good Luck on Your Journey!

###

About the Author

Mohammed Musthafa Soukath Ali

SCJP, LOMA 286, PMP, PSM, PSPO, SA, SPC

Musthafa is the author of the #1 Best Selling book Scrum Narrative and PSM Exam Guide in smashwords.com. He is ranked as one of the Tata Consultancy Services (TCS) Global Top Project Planners, acting as specialist coach for complex IT Application Development projects. He is also the external Management Capability Adviser for some of the Tata Group Companies. He is a designated Agile Software Delivery Expert, having consulted with 10+ global customers. He published 9 papers in conferences with two international speaker invitations in Berlin, Germany and in Spain. He is one of the Subject Matter Experts in the TCS Corporate Agile Think-tank. Currently he works out of Chennai, India.

You can connect with the author through his LinkedIn network: https://in.linkedin.com/in/mohammed-musthafa-soukath-ali-9a857762

About the Editor-in-Chief

Samantha Mason

PSM, CSM

Samantha began as a software engineer at Altsys Corporation, later acquired by Macromedia, working on the graphics program FreeHand. Her teams worked in an Agile way before the term was coined. Her expertise in real-world development provides a unique advantage in editing and presenting information aimed at those new to Agile developments. Samantha is also the editor of the #1 Best Selling book Scrum Narrative and PSM Exam Guide in smashwords.com. Being a trained facilitator for The Knowledge Academy, she has access to students new to Scrum and Agile and their interest in SAFe®, which allows her to continuously update publications to address ambiguous areas. Currently she works out of Mequon, Wisconsin.

You can connect with the editor through her LinkedIn network:

https://in.linkedin.com/in/samantha-mason-956b069b

##

SAFe® and Scaled Agile Framework® are registered trademarks of Scaled Agile, Inc.

Made in the USA
Coppell, TX
21 July 2022

80260328R00064